WRITING TO WRITE

WRITING TO WRITE

Process, Collaboration, Communication

DANA C. ELDER
EASTERN WASHINGTON UNIVERSITY

MACMILLAN PUBLISHING COMPANY

New York

Editor: Barbara Heinssen
Production Supervisor: Ros Herion Freese
Text Designer: Ros Herion Freese
Illustrations: Wellington Studios

Cartoon Credits: "The Far Side" cartoons by Gary Larson (pp. vii, 1, 95,
111, and 149) are reprinted by permission of Chronicle Features, San
Francisco, CA. "The Far Side" cartoons by Gary Larson (pp. 31, 41, 57, 77, and
163) are copyright 1984, 1985, 1986, 1987 Universal Press Syndicate; reprinted
with permission; all rights reserved.

This book was set in Melior by Digitype, Inc.

Macmillan Publishing Company
866 Third Avenue, New York, New York 10022

Library of Congress Cataloging-in-Publication Data

Elder, Dana C.
    Writing to write: process, collaboration, communication / Dana C. Elder.
        p.   cm.
    Includes index.
    1. English language — Rhetoric.   I. Title
    PE1408.E413   1990
    808'.042 — dc20   89-35047
                                                                    CIP

Printing: 1 2 3 4 5 6 7   Year: 0 1 2 3 4 5 6

In memory of *Blanche Iva Derby*, my grandmother,
who often advised and rarely judged

PREFACE

"So, then . . . Would that be 'us
the people' or 'we the people?'"

For years I sought a composition textbook that was only a rhetoric, one that was focused on guiding students—through principles, examples, and practice—toward better and better written
communication skills. For several reasons I sought a short book,
one that would be a resource for me and my students rather than
a complete course, one that would allow me also to select and use
a supplementary reader or grammar text—depending on the

skills and needs of the student with whom I worked — and not overly tax the students' pocketbooks. *Writing to Write* is such a book. It is a collection of integrated resources for teachers and students of writing; it includes (1) a communication model that helps students to think of writing in terms of *practical* communication goals, (2) a skill-building journal that encourages fluency and discovery, (3) numerous peer group learning strategies, (4) suggestions and techniques for prewriting, writing, and rewriting, and (5) accessible options for organizing written discourse to meet clear communication goals. All of these components are presented as *resources*, as activities that writers *may* rather than *must* utilize.

The intended audience for this text is entry-level college writers. With the appropriate supplementary materials, this text could also be used effectively with less skilled writers. Many of the students that we might place in either of these groups have had few opportunities and little motivation to write. Most of the writing that they have done has been school-sponsored. They tend, therefore, to see writing as a necessary but somewhat painful feature of education. Many believe that the only audience for their writing is the teacher and that the only purpose for writing is a good grade. These attitudes, I believe, inhibit their growth as writers, as communicators.

Unlike some of the writing textbooks now available, *Writing to Write* includes student writing and multiple drafts of some student essays which illustrate useful writing and rewriting techniques. This text also draws upon both classical and contemporary approaches to teaching communication skills, and it reinforces key concepts in every chapter. These features make the book more accessible and especially useful to less experienced composition instructors. The brevity of the text gives both veteran and beginning teachers room to teach.

Three assumptions permeate the whole text and, I hope, will guide its use in the classroom. The first assumption is that people write to communicate, that classroom instruction in writing is a path to effective written communication skills which will serve those instructed throughout their lives, in school and out. The second is that people learn to write by writing and rewriting.

Suggestions offered by the instructor, other students, and the writer to him- or herself during the process of writing an essay accelerate this learning. The third assumption is that mistakes are evidence of risk taking; they highlight those areas where the student needs more practice and more guidance. People make errors when they attempt to do things they do not already know how to do; therefore, errors should be seen as opportunities for additional instruction and learning.

I will also share with you an attitude that I hope is demonstrated by this whole book. In the fourth century B.C., Aristotle went to Plato's Academy in Athens. Classical scholars believe that he went to the Academy not to study philosophy but to "live" philosophy. He wanted not to know what was right but to do what was right. In the same way that many people go to school not to learn things but to learn how to learn, so they can make learning itself an ongoing part of their lives; they want to be learners, to live learning. In the same way, I hope that many of those who read this book will be writers, will make writing an ongoing part of their lives.

Writing is more than just a skill required of students. People who can write, write. Writing, by its very nature, becomes a vehicle that carries them toward clearer and more sophisticated thinking. Furthermore, writing skills are communication skills. A person who practices the organization and presentation of ideas and opinions in writing learns to speak more effectively — actually becomes a better communicator.

The *Instructor's Manual* available with the text suggests a few, but by no means all, approaches to using this textbook. I hope that those who read the manual will perceive the suggestions as options, and use those which best meet the needs of the educational situations in which they find themselves. The classroom teacher designs and develops his or her course. He or she is the only person in a position to do so.

This is a concise book but by no means a simple one. It asks for imagination, collaboration, and complex thinking. Good communication skills are its principle concern. My fondest wish is that this book in fact practices what it preaches, that it communicates.

ACKNOWLEDGMENTS

Thanks go to the following reviewers, who offered many helpful suggestions during the manuscript stage: Donna Alden, University of New Mexico; Debra Journet, University of Louisville; Ellen A. Knodt, Pennsylvania State University—Ogontz; William Peirce, Prince George's Community College; Fred Reynolds, Old Dominion University; Howard B. Tinberg, Bristol Community College. A very heartfelt thank you goes to William E. Sheidley, University of Connecticut, whose honesty and insights were especially useful to me.

DANA C. ELDER

TO THE STUDENT

This is a self-help book. It is also a help-one-another book. The experts say that a writer's first and most important audience is the writer him- or herself. Inside their heads, people often talk to themselves before sharing their words and thoughts with anyone. It follows that they could also write to themselves. Some people imagine conversations between themselves and their friends or themselves and their boss—guessing what those conversations will be like when they take place. But in addition to talking to themselves, people talk to others; they communicate. Imagining yourself communicating is not communicating. Communicating takes two or more people. So you need to work on your writing skills with other people. You need a real audience, real talkers and readers to write and read and talk with.

So how do you use this book? You read and talk and write, and write, and write. There will be many suggestions along the way. The suggestions have been organized to help in three important ways—preparing yourself to write, getting that first full version of your essay down on paper, and then making that essay as good as it can be.

Learning to write is more like learning to cook. You might have a recipe for spaghetti sauce, but, like writing, every time you make a spaghetti sauce it is somehow different. The variables—ingredients, types of equipment (pans, pots, conventional [electric or gas] or microwave oven), how much time you have, and how many people you are trying to feed—all influence the meal you finally serve. Writing is like that. Every time you write, it will be different. You may have weeks or minutes to complete the task. You may use pen or personal computer. You may be writing to your parents, your boss, or to Ford Motor Company. You may be writing to yourself.

Also, like cooking, what you plan to make and what you end up making might be radically different. That doesn't necessarily mean that what you end up with is not edible (even delicious) or readable (even well written). To extend the analogy, cooking can be an art. Not all meals are fast food. But to be really good at preparing meals, you have to prepare many of them. The same is true of essays. In neither cooking nor writing is there one "right way" to get the job done. On the other hand there are, I believe, certain assumptions that a writer should make.

Chapter 1 offers strategies for getting started, for putting your ideas and opinions in writing without worrying about grades or spelling errors. It asks that you write ten or fifteen minutes a day, four days a week, about ideas or issues that interest you. By doing this, you will benefit in several ways. Most importantly, by writing regularly you will get used to writing. This practice will help you to write more quickly; it will actually make the muscles in your writing hand stronger or improve your keyboarding skills. Writing regularly will also give you opportunities to try out ideas and opinions. For most people, writing becomes a way to find, shape, and polish thoughts.

Remember, too, that the daily writing asked of you in Chapter 1 is never meant to be graded or judged. That's not what it's for. It is for you. It is a safe place for you to practice writing.

Chapter 2 presents one pattern or *process* for producing a complete essay. It lets you practice prewriting (getting ready to write), writing (getting your ideas and opinions organized and down on paper), and rewriting (making what you have written even better). Chapter 2 is a kind of miniversion of the whole process of writing presented in this book.

Chapter 3 is about communicating in writing. Thinking about communication itself, and about the best ways to write what you want to say to the person or people you want to say it to, is part of getting started. Thinking is one of the most important parts of preparing yourself to write an essay. Thinking about communication makes a person a better communicator, and not just in writing. The ideas presented in Chapter 3 may also help you to speak more easily and effectively.

Chapter 4 offers more strategies for preparing yourself to write. All people have times when their minds feel empty, when none of their thoughts about a subject seem very interesting. This is especially common when someone else tells writers what to write about. When writers get stuck, they can either give up or start playing with ideas — hoping to discover some that will help. Chapter 4 contains some strategies for finding and playing with ideas.

Chapter 5 presents another way of looking at how essays are put together. Written language can accomplish many things — telling a story, sharing information, and offering advice are just a few examples. This chapter suggests that many essays are made up of combinations of different types of written language and of distinct but related units, or clusters of related paragraphs. The idea is for the writer to choose and create units for an essay that best meet the needs of the writing situation.

After you have done the writing, talking, and thinking asked of you in Chapters 1–5, you will be better able to prepare to write a longer essay. Chapter 6 contains, therefore, case studies of other students preparing to write essays. There is no single right way to prepare to write an essay, but there are many good strategies for completing that preparation.

Chapter 7 asks that you use all of the skills you have practiced in the previous chapters as you prepare to write and then actually write a draft of a longer essay. Then it offers answers to the question, "What next?" After you have written that first full version of your essay, then what? The answer is to share the early version of your essay with real readers. This can be frightening, but it doesn't have to be. If those real readers know how to help rather than judge you, then their comments can guide you in your efforts to make the essay better. Just as importantly, you will be learning to make helpful suggestions to other writers about their essays.

Chapter 8 offers strategies for making good essays even better. You will be asked to work through your essays one more time, this time looking even more closely at the needs of your audience. For example, many people believe that it is easier to write or rewrite an introduction and a conclusion to an essay *after* the essay is written. This makes sense. How can you write an effective introduction to an essay before you know what the essay will communicate? How can you write the best possible conclusion before you have written your best possible essay?

Next comes a short *Letter to the Student* about learning to speak and write Standard American English. This is the language shared by educated Americans; it is also a language of international trade and politics. Standard American English is a powerful resource both in and out of educational environments.

So how does one use this book? One writes and shares one's writing with others. One gives and receives helpful suggestions about writing and then uses those suggestions. A person becomes, in the process, a better and better writer.

One learns to write by writing. Since writing essays is difficult, some mistakes will be made while learning to write them. So what? Expect to make mistakes. Learn from them. If you can think of mistakes as necessary parts of learning, you already have a head start.

Last summer my son had his sixteenth birthday. In the state where we live, sixteen-year-olds can legally start learning to drive automobiles. So I picked up a booklet on traffic rules, and my son memorized it. In addition, I told him as much about driving a car as I could think of; in fact, I told him all I could think of about twenty times. "Take the car out of gear before turning the ignition switch," I told him. "Let the clutch out slowly while slowly pressing on the gas pedal," I said. Then we sat in the driveway in my little white pickup and practiced changing gears, signaling turns, and adjusting the rearview mirror.

Next I told him another twenty times everything I had learned about driving these past twenty years. He was polite and patient, but when he started quoting my own advice back to me, I knew it was time to hit the road.

So we went out to a quiet country road, and he got behind the wheel. He put the car in neutral and started it. By this time he had heard every thought I'd ever had about clutches and gears about a hundred times. Even so, he stalled the engine nine times before the pickup started jerking down the gravel road.

He had listened to me lecture about turning radius. He should have been an expert. But making his very first turn he actually missed the road and hit a four-by-four fencepost.

The point is this: People can hear writing strategies explained. They can read all about writing. They can talk about "what it takes" for hours, months, or years. But the learning starts when the pen hits the page. When my son hit the fence, I was disappointed but not really surprised. "There's so much to do," he said. "Put on the signal, look for other cars, put in the clutch, change the gear, turn the wheel. . . ."

"Yes," I replied. "Take it out of gear, start it up, and let's go hit another fence."

Like learning to drive, learning to write is hard work. Good writing skills take time to develop. I hear remarks like, "I'm going to be an accountant, so I don't really need to write well" or "If I can just pass freshman English, I won't have to write anymore." Neither of these attitudes is realistic. Many people think that working toward quality writing skills helps people learn to think more quickly and more clearly and makes them better communicators. I agree. Writing and reading do more than help a person get good grades in school; they actually help people live better.

Remember that writing *is* a process. It takes time and effort. Remember, too, that each writing project *always* takes more time and more effort than you think it will before you start on it. You should give each writing project your best effort and as much time as you can, and then feel good about it. People learn to write by writing. With practice and guidance, you and the people with whom you write will become better and better writers.

CONTENTS

Chapter 1

PEN MEETS PAPER
Writing Every Day

8-23 Larson · Chronicle Features, 1982

"Look! Look, gentlemen! . . . Purple mountains! Spacious skies! Fruited plains! . . . Is someone writing this down?"

DAILY WRITING ASSIGNMENTS

People learn by doing. This maxim is true of all areas of learning and applies to every skill. A person can stand beside the pool admiring the blue-green water for eternity without learning how to swim. Sooner or later that person has to get wet.

1

While almost everyone would agree that a novice plumber or swimmer has to start plumbing or swimming, our culture perpetuates a strange myth about writing. For some good reasons, writing is often thought of as art, and many people think art simply happens. It doesn't. Somebody in history might have just sat down and painted a masterpiece, but I doubt it. Someone who had not written much before might have written a bestseller in a weekend, but I doubt that, too. There are many examples of the opposite happening. Tolstoy wrote *War and Peace* at least seven times—and *War and Peace* is over fifteen hundred long pages long. No one simply becomes a writer overnight.

Writing is complex. But it can be divided into less complex parts, and those parts can be practiced. Fortunately, any writing a person does helps to improve that person's writing skills. It is likely that by writing short stories a bank manager will learn to compose better business letters and that writing many personal letters will help a scriptwriter to create better scripts. The key, once again, is practice.

So let's practice. I suggest, as others have mentioned before, that once a person decides to write, he or she should do so on a regular basis. I further suggest the following pattern of writing at least four days a week; the guidelines are simple:

1. Write every day. For many people, it is easier to write in a classroom with other people. Some prefer to write all by themselves. It is a good idea to do both.
2. Don't worry or even think about spelling, punctuation, or grammar (discounting these concerns is harder than you think).
3. Write quickly. Do not spend a lot of time on the "right" word or the "perfect" sentence. Try to think of daily writing tasks as "word races." Your goal is to get down as many words as possible as quickly as possible.
4. Write for ten to fifteen minutes, and keep writing until the time is up (use a kitchen timer if it helps).

Following are the daily writing tasks.

Monday: "What I really think about . . ."

There are two ways to select topics for Monday writing. The first is for each writer to choose something he or she has been thinking about — painting the house, asking for a raise, the AIDS epidemic, a tax the writer is tired of paying, or the rising cost of produce at the supermarket. In this way, each writer chooses something that he or she cares about.

The second way to choose topics for Mondays is for the whole class to do it. In class, people name possible topics. Small topics work better than large ones. For example, everyone has ideas and opinions about borrowing or lending money, doing homework, maintaining a car, or being polite. In ten or fifteen minutes, a person could write about such topics. Large subjects, like the national debt, war, love, or religion are for books — thick books. Experience suggests that nobody can write what he or she really thinks about war or love in fifteen minutes. On the other hand, most people can write what they really think about parking tickets in that amount of time.

A compromise would be to use both strategies for choosing topics. Early in the course, the class members could make a list of Monday topics. To save time, the instructor could choose items from the list for the first two Mondays of the school term. Everyone would write about these. The third Monday each writer would choose a different topic. Then the instructor (or the students themselves) could select two more topics. This way every third Monday the topics are self-selected.

However the Monday topics are selected, on Mondays each writer writes about that Monday's topic for ten or fifteen minutes without stopping. Writers who run out of things to write should rewrite the last word they have written until they think of something else to write. The point is to keep writing. Most people find that their writing hand gets tired when they write without stopping. This is normal; people actually need this exercise to build up the writing muscles in their hands. This writing can also be done on a word processor. What is lost in terms of muscle development is gained in terms of speed and keyboarding skills.

Every writer should try to be honest. Don't write down the thoughts of experts you've read or the opinions of other people. Write what *you* think. Some people don't know what they think about something until they write about it, so writing often clarifies thinking. It also helps to develop what experts call *style*. Part of what people call *style* is that feeling when reading something that someone is really saying what he or she thinks or feels.

The three following examples are real; they were written by people who were trying to communicate something. Each still contains some grammar and punctuation errors, but for the writers and for readers, each says something. In each, the writer is playing with his or her own thoughts.

Examples of Monday Writing

MONDAY EXAMPLE #1:

```
"What I really think about debt."
```

Debt can come in many forms. This is something
everyone should avoid to have peace of mind.
    Debt is something I would always try to avoid. The
debt or owing somebody something has always bothered me
and always puts a heavy burden inside my mind. This heavy
burden seems to consist of anxiety, time and worry. Debt
always has a way of controlling a person. There is always
a time factor and this is where the person in debt is not
in control. I sometimes have seen such cases and the
person in debt not only ends up feeling bad, depressed but
could also end up losing the trust of friends. There the
best policy is to evade debt in anyway one can.

                                            Sidin T.
                                            121 words
```
```

MONDAY EXAMPLE #2:

''What I really think about debt.''

Being in debt means one thing, owing someone money. My opinion on being in debt is split because it can either work for you or work against you. When you take out a loan or receive a line of credit, your main intention is to purchase something. Purchasing item on credit allow you to enjoy the product now, instead of waiting until you've saved the money. There are alot of people though that go over board on their spending. It's very easy to try to buy something on credit because you never actually hand over any money. Until of course, you receive the bill in the mail. Say for instance you have many credit cards, each of which has a high balance. Unless you make alot of money and can pay off each one, you'll probably be paying the minimum payment on each. And in the long run you'll have payed alot of interest.

If you control your spending and manage your money being in debt can work for you. It can allow you to buy a home, a car, or even start a business of your own. Being in debt is what you make of it. If you don't get carried away it'll allow you to enjoy many things.

Curt G.
207 words

MONDAY EXAMPLE #3:

''What I really think about debt.''

To me, ''debt'' has two distinct, different characteristics. One is for ''you owe me,'' the other is one of ''I owe you.''

The first, "you owe me," is almost non-existent in my life, not because no one owed me anything, but because when I do something for someone or give someone something I do and give as a favor, not something that has to be repaid to me. I do things keeping in mind that I do not expect direct repayment.

The concept of "I owe you" that I have is different than most other people's concept also. When someone does something for me or gives me something, I will attempt direct repayment. But if direct repayment is not requested, I will repay that person through different means such as helping on other projects. For example, if a person gives me money when I really need it, I might repay them by helping them with their homework or housework project, rather than paying them back with money in return.

Also, if the person knows me well enough, they would understand that I have a "pass it on" attitude. If I receive help when it is needed, I in turn help others, not the original helper, and hope that they in turn will in turn help someone else when they need help.

So there it is. If I help others, I expect, and do not wait for a repayment from them, for I could get it from somewhere else. And if I get help from others, I am most likely to "pass it on." I believe you get what you give. That is why I enjoy "sending out" alot of help with "no strings attached," for this is what I like to receive.

Deborah L.
279 words

Comments on These Examples of Monday Writing: The thoughts expressed are fairly universal; each of us thinks and probably worries about debt. What these three Monday writing examples share, however, is that each contains a few of the writer's ideas and opinions. It is risky to write what you really think. People think that sharing what they think makes them vulnerable, so even *trying* to write what they really think is risky. In addition, many times a writer attempting to be honest about his or her own thoughts will not capture them. This is normal. Maybe one out of every five attempts will be a partial success, but so what? If one out of ten helps the writer to look at a problem or concern differently, then all ten efforts are worth the time and effort.

The idea is to keep your mind open and your expectations low, and just keep writing.

Tuesday: "The letter I should probably write"

Every person should write more letters. You don't have to look for occasions to write letters — they seem to come up all the time. Is there someone you should thank for a favor or a gift? Is somebody's birthday coming up? Did the credit card billing company make another mistake? Did one of your friends move to New Zealand or Korea? Postage is cheap; long distance phone charges are not.

On Tuesdays, then, write a letter to somebody. Write like you would talk to this person. Mention some interests you share and *always* include some good news. Most people think of letters as welcome gifts.

Some people expect a letter in return when they write. Don't. If you wait for a return letter before writing to the same person again, you might wait a long time. Don't keep track; nobody owes you a letter in return. You are writing to communicate, not to make somebody else write back.

Most people find it easy to write to someone they know. Look at the following letters written by students.

Examples of Tuesday Writing

TUESDAY EXAMPLE #1:

''The letter I should probably write.''

Dear Mom,
    All seems to be going just fine. I have gotten
settled into my apartment. It really isn't so bad except
that the building is old and abused. I guess I can't
really expect alot for $150 a month.
    Weather up here has been really nice. Today was
somewhat over-cast but it was clearing off before I sat
down to write this letter.
    Classes seem to be just about what I wanted for my
first semester back.
    Willi and I went into town last Sunday and goofed
off. We stopped by Wade and Junel's and had quite a few
good laughs. They were very hung over from the night
before. They swore they would never touch alcohol again.
    It really seems strange at having to be in a
classroom. It doesn't seem like that long ago, but when
you stop and think about it--Bang! Where did the time go?
    I seem to be getting along fine. Not lonely or
anything yet!

                                              Love,
                                              Mark
                                         163 words

TUESDAY EXAMPLE #2:

''The letter I should probably write.''

To: Jin S.
    How are you? As compared with the weather of Seoul,
we have had changeable weather. I mean temperature

difference is very changeable between day and night.
Most of American university students don't take
summer school. They get a job for helping tuition,
living expense, and so on. So our campus is somewhat
inactive.

Yesterday, we started summer school. This is the
third quarter for me, as you know. So I have many
problems, specially, speech and listening. I changed my
major, so I had to read the textbook before the class
during 2 quarters. If I didn't prepare for the class at
all, I didn't listen at all.

I think our program about English isn't good. We
studied just reading and grammar in high school, not
listening, speech. In order to adapt oneself to new
circumstances, I think the most important thing is
communication and listening. Some people told me that
making friends with someone was the good way for you to
improve English. But at first I didn't have much time, and
I was shy, and I had a little homesick. Now I am more
active than first quarter.

I work at Tawanka (school cafeteria). It is very
hard. But after working, it is worthwhile, because it
helps me to buy something. After this quarter I try to
make friends and I will visit L.A. My friend lives in
L.A., and maybe you know her. I would like to know many
things from travel. What do you think about my plan?

My English professor gives us writing letter as the
homework. I think my English skill isn't good and I know
about that. I want to improve my English from this
class. Of course, this class is hard to me, but I do my
best. I would like to know your life of these days. If you
have a little time, could you write a letter to me?

Good-bye and take care.

Sincerely,
Hey-Jung K.
320 words

TUESDAY EXAMPLE #3:

''The letter I should probably write.''

Dear Mom,

Howdy peg leg! How goes it back at the ranch?

Things have been pretty hectic around here. I still haven't gotten any rest after our trip to Canada.

I have 3 classes right in a row. I go go go from 9:30 a.m. to 2 p.m. No breaks.

I think this chemistry class, (the one for Boneheads) Chem. 120, is going to be good for me since I have missed out on every chemistry class in high school. This will give me a good background if I have to go further into chemistry. I'll at least have gotten the basics of it even if I don't have to go any further.

Got my Pell grant check today. I thought that I would owe the school some money like last time. But this time I got a whole $211.00 back. That was because they didn't take out the rent like they usually do. Wow! A lot it will help having $211. Too bad my rent for this quarter will be $350. Well, I know I can cover the rest with what I get from the Tribe.

About the Tribe. Who won the elections? Did our favorite cage rattler Lou get back in? I sure hope so! Those old Fogies need a little spice to liven them up!

Well, well, well, well, well, well, well, well, I'm not one to repeat myself, but I had to do that because Elder said to go non-stop stop even if we drew a blank on what to say. So naturally, I also interpreted it as to go non-stop if I have trouble figuring out how to say it.

On with business, business, business. I finally got Chuck's insurance payment sent off today. I also got sent off the corrections to my Pell forms.

Those idiots! Why do they have to complain about

blank lines if they tell you to leave it blank if the
questions do not apply to me?
Oh well, such is life. Have a good one Mom.

Love ya!
Deborah L.
351 words

TUESDAY EXAMPLE #4:

"The letter I should probably write."

Dear Nike,
For the last seven years I've been using your shoes
for Track and Field competition, and for the last seven
years I've had nothing but good luck with them, until last
weekend. Last Saturday I was competing in a college
indoor meet at Eastern University. I was running down the
runway during the Triple-Jump competition and right in
the middle of my jump, as my right foot hit the ground, my
"Nike T.J.-60" tore apart. This caused me to fall and
tear my "Nike" running tights. Luckily I was not hurt;
unluckily I did poorly on the rest of my jumps wearing a
taped-up shoe.
I have seen several guys fall on indoor tracks
wearing running tights and never get holes in them. As
for the shoes, I've used them in only eight meets so they
were practically new.
I feel the least you could do about this is replace
these defective items with products I can have confidence
in. There are too many things to think about during a
track meet; I shouldn't have to worry about my shoes
holding together. My shoe size is nine and a half, and
medium-long in the running tights.

Sincerely Yours,
Clint J.
198 words

Comments on These Examples of Tuesday Writing: These four letters may or may not have been sent. Sending a letter is satisfying; it makes you feel like you have done something. Letters to friends reinforce friendships. Letters to companies are usually responded to. Experience suggests that calls to companies on the phone to complain about a product or clarify a billing error do not work. It is just too easy to ignore a phone call. Letters, on the other hand, are hard to ignore. They become a kind of record. Companies, in general, are eager to respond to written consumer complaints or compliments. They have a responsibility to do so. But even if they don't, expressing concerns in writing helps a person feel better about those concerns; the person has done something.

When writing to a company, it is wise to present yourself as concerned rather than angry. It is also smart to praise the company's products in some way. You want them to read your letter. Even if the company never responds to your letter, you have won. You have expressed yourself, and you have expressed your concerns whether you send the letter or not.

Wednesday: "Responding to something you have read"

On Wednesday, write a ten- to fifteen-minute response to something you've read in a newspaper or magazine. The best way to improve your writing skills is to write, but the second best way is to read. Written language is in some ways different from spoken language. Reading helps people become more aware of these differences. Read three or four articles before selecting one to write about.

What you choose to read is less important than you might think. You should read what interests you. If motorcycles are your passion, read about motorcycles. If you find fashion fascinating, read about fashion. The first goal is *quantity*: read often. The second goal, though not as important as the first, is *variety*: read several different kinds of material. You should read a newspaper at least once a week, even if you only read the comics and the sports page. You would be smart to read a news magazine about once a week as well; otherwise, all your information about what is going on in the country and in the world is pre-digested. News items on television tend to be short. You seem to get the tip rather than the iceberg. Some people think that TV news contains too few facts and too much opinion. You need enough facts to build your own opinions.

So, on Wednesdays read something and respond to it in writing. Spend about five minutes paraphrasing or summarizing what you have read; then spend another five or ten minutes responding to that information.

It is smart to make a photocopy of the article you have read, and write on the top of it the name of the magazine or newspaper in which you found the article and the date it was published; then staple this photocopy to your written response. This step enables you to take a quotation from the article at a later time — quickly and easily.

Read the following examples of Wednesday writing. Ignore the spelling, grammar, and punctuation errors you find, and look instead at the ideas and opinions expressed. Identify those ideas you could write about.

Examples of Wednesday Writing

WEDNESDAY EXAMPLE #1:

''Responding to something you have read.''

I was looking at a cartoon which showed the famous Uncle Sam running away from the Japanese who were chasing him. I read an article in Time a few weeks ago which said that foreign investors are buying American companies and at the top of the list were the Japanese, along with the English, Germans, Dutch, Swedes, Canadians and Australians.

I was surprised when I read the part of the article which said the amount of money that was invested; those

numbers were billions and trillions of dollars. In my
language, we call these kinds of numbers "star numbers"
since they are so hard to think about or even to imagine.
I find them hard to imagine.

I wonder what is going to happen in, let's say,
twenty or thirty years? I'd like to see if there is still
any company in American hands at all.

It seems that the only way to avoid the fall of the
American economy is to cut those foreign investors and to
pass a law that prohibits foreign countries from
investing in the American economy, or at least to pass a
law that will limit how many companies a foreign country
can buy.

Mohsen S.
199 words

WEDNESDAY EXAMPLE #2:

Response to the article,
"District 81 abolishes corporal punishment."

I believe the abolishment of corporal punishment is
very stupid. When a young student does something wrong,
like against the rules and/or the law, then he should be
hacked. When a person gets a hack it not only hurts but is
also very embarrassing. They shouldn't change a rule
that everyone else grew up with because it's no different
now than it was twenty years ago.

I remember when I was in the seventh grade. That's
when I got my first and also last hack. I forgot to do my
homework and the class rule was if you didn't do your
homework then you had to get a hack. Everyone knew I had
to get a hack and that made me feel real stupid! After
that day I did my homework every day. I feel that I really
learned a lesson because I was embarrassed, and the hack
also hurt like hell!

I know that most teachers wouldn't spank a student

without a good reason, so why take the right of spanking
students away from teachers? To me corporal punishment is
a good way to discipline students.

James L.
188 words

WEDNESDAY EXAMPLE #3:

The article that I read is a controversy between two
businesses. A small vegetarian restaurant is opened by
two men. Bernard Shapiro and Daniel Prather are both
vegetarians, and wanted a restaurant with not only the
convenience of fast food but also have healthy food. They
called their restaurant McDharma's and McDonald's
decided to take action. The two partners decided to
settle out of court for an undisclosed amount of money.
They then painted the international symbol for
''forbidden'' over the ''Mc'' on their sign. McDonalds
didn't accept it and are suing again.
My opinion on this is that I also would be upset if
someone used part of my idea to further their own profits.
Everybody that goes into business should use fresh and
new ideas. I know from personal experience that its not
the name of your restaurant that sells food. Its the
quality of the food and service that brings customers
back. So if your going to open a business, be an original,
not an imitator.

Curt G.
171 words

WEDNESDAY EXAMPLE #4:

Article: <u>National Enquirer</u>, July 5, 1988

Summary: Women executives do better than men because
they are able to gain a person's confidence faster than a

man can. Also, women, by nature, are more apt to work at
getting along and listen to other's concerns. Fewer
women owned new businesses fail in the first five year
"danger" period.

      Opinion: At first reading this, the article could
make one like me feel good! It sounds good! It sounds
encouraging! It makes it sound like one such as myself
would have a real chance to be a success in the business
world!

      <u>But</u>! Reality comes back. What the article does not
mention is the fact that women almost never make it to the
high executive ranks. The only clue is where it is stated
that 31 middle-level were a group of the people
interviewed.

      I recall an article (from somewhere) that I read a
couple of months ago that stated there was only one
Fortune 500 company that had a woman as a high ranking
executive.

      This article could be misleading to many people! If
one stops to think about it, they would realize that the
BEST women have been able to do (as a whole) so far is to
make it to the mid-management level. The reason for this
is because (I found in another article) men are the ones
in the higher ranks--and they promote their own.

      Do they have a fear of us women? Is it really "our
place" to be of lower business ranking? Do "they" not
trust "us"? Are we really so stupid that we cannot
handle high executive positions? Could we really be
better than them if we can ever get to the top?

Deborah L.
282 words

Comments on These Examples of Wednesday Writing: Reading
is good for you. Trying to figure out what something you read
means to you and to your life is very good for you. When you try
to write a response to something you have read and don't really
capture your ideas in writing, that is good. Your own confusion is

good; it forces you to think again. If you read one of your Wednesday writings and say to yourself, "That's not what I think," you can always write it again. A person can speak without really thinking; but writing encourages and often demands thinking. You can always rewrite; respeaking is difficult.

The most common problem I see in Wednesday writing is dullness. People tend to think that what some other author has written is more important than what they can write. This is not true. The best way to avoid dullness is to include specific details and examples from your own experience in your Wednesday writing. When you agree with what you have read, write out examples from your own knowledge or experience that support what this other author has written. When you disagree, include details and examples from your own life that make you think differently.

Thursday: "Rethink"

In a way, writing about something forces you to realize ideas and opinions about that something or to express ideas and opinions you already have. The writer who wrote about avoiding debt whenever possible (Monday Example #1) thought that having debts gave someone else control over the debtor. The man who wrote about Nike products believed that those products should be more durable.

Not every piece of daily writing that a person does will contain honest ideas or opinions, but every essay should. For most people, *an essay is a writer's ideas and opinions about something and the reasons that writer has those ideas and opinions.*

On Thursdays, then, read what you have written so far during that week. Look for an idea or opinion that surprises, pleases, or intrigues you. When you read a line and say to yourself, "I wrote that?" you have found what you are looking for. If nothing you have written surprises you, pick an idea or opinion that still interests you.

Once you have chosen an opinion or idea, write for another ten or fifteen minutes about it. This time consciously include examples, details, and facts to back up what you are writing. Let the reader know why you think what you think. The reader doesn't have to agree, but it is your job to help that reader understand. Facts, examples, and details add weight to your thoughts and opinions, and they allow a reader to see where your ideas and opinions are coming from.

Friday: "Writer's Choice" (Optional)

If there is a particular kind of writing that you really enjoy doing—poetry or short stories or short written sketches of funny things that happen to you—then write an extra day each week. Because there is no assigned daily writing on Fridays, Fridays would be good days to do this. If you choose to do this additional writing, do the same kind of writing for at least three weeks. Don't, for example, write a poem one week and a story the next. Since you are doing this only for yourself, have fun doing it. Writing doesn't have to be painful or even serious. People often find serious ideas and opinions in daily writing efforts that they intended to make playful or even silly.

WHAT TO DO WITH ALL THIS DAILY WRITING

After five weeks or five thousand words, you will unavoidably be a better writer than you are now. Don't be concerned if sometimes the words flow faster or slower—this is to be expected. Keep all of this writing in a notebook in the order in which you wrote it.

Five weeks of daily writing is a minimum. One must write at least that long before seeing much improvement. Ten weeks of daily writing is recommended, and fifteen weeks is desirable, but the more writing the better, so don't quit writing. The following are a few suggestions about what to do with this first series of writing efforts:

Responding to Daily Writing Assignments

1. Monday entries are just for you. You are writing to yourself and for yourself. Read through these and check to see if you are really writing what you think. If you have trouble writing what you think, try writing the opposite of what you think — play the part of devil's advocate.
2. Tuesday entries, the letters, can be sent — perhaps not all of them, but some of them should weave their way through the postal system and into the hand of the person to whom you are writing. It is almost as fun to send a letter as it is to receive one.
3. Wednesday entries serve mainly as places to record, store, and play with ideas and opinions.
4. Thursday writing, "Rethinks," should be shared with other students. Two writers can exchange "Rethinks." I ask that neither of you correct the other's spelling, punctuation, or grammar. Instead, limit your responses to the following four comments:
   a. *"Add an example."* When as reader you have some idea of what the writer means but aren't quite sure, an example is needed.
   b. *"Add details."* Many writers tell the reader instead of showing what they mean. Emotion words often tell rather than show. Instead of writing "He was happy," describe what his face and hands were doing when he was happy. Instead of "It was a great car," describe how the vehicle looks, smells, sounds, and feels.

Look for a minute at the following examples. On the left are short statements of opinion. On the right are the same opinions, but the writers have included details and examples that help the reader to understand the opinions.

"My money doesn't seem to go as far this year as it did last year."	"Electricity costs 22% more this year than last, a chicken I could have bought for $0.49 a pound this time last year is now $1.09 a pound, and my wife and I quit buying beef entirely."
"I work too much."	"After putting in forty-five hours a week on the job and an hour and a half each day on cooking, cleaning, or laundry, I just can't seem to get out and dig those weeds out of the backyard garden."
"My daughter doesn't know how to treat cats yet."	"Alice, my towheaded five-year-old with all the freckles, carries the cat with its head locked between the crook of her elbow and her body. Then she thinks the cat doesn't like her."

c. *"Write about this again."* The reader should make this suggestion when the reader thinks the writer really cares about what he or she is writing.

d. *"This sounds honest."* Make this comment when what you are reading "sounds" like a real voice speaking about real concerns.

All four of these responses are mostly for the writer's information. The writer needs to have someone else to remind him or her to use examples and details more often and to suggest which ideas and observations need to be expanded. Sharing Thursday notebook entries should happen regularly, perhaps once a week. But even without a writing partner, the writer can offer these four responses to him- or herself.

Most people like to be praised. It is wise to praise a piece of writing by pointing to places in it where the writer uses interesting examples or specific details. Write *"good example"* or *"excellent details"* next to these places. Perhaps the highest praise is when somebody says a piece of writing is *"honest."* A reader just seems to know when people have written what they really think. Writing honestly is genuine communication. In fact, by writing regularly and honestly, people can learn about themselves.

The following is a Thursday "Rethink" on which are written four responses. Usually it is wise to write only two to four responses on a short piece of writing. The idea is to help the writer, not to dwell upon his or her weaknesses. This journal entry is not wonderful, but it does include details and examples, and the writer seems to be saying what she really thinks about something that has affected her life. The reader's job is to respond to the writing in ways that help the writer make it better.

THURSDAY "RETHINK":

My Attitude about Cocaine

This sounds honest

> Cocaine destroys a person's life. The use of cocaine seems to be all around me. It doesn't seem like I can have a conversation with an acquaintance or a group of people without the topic of cocaine coming up. People ask where they can buy some or talk about the good stuff that they snorted the previous night. If they are trying to get a congenial response from me about this topic, they soon find out differently. Most people who know

me well know better than to even
bring up the topic. The word itself
conjures up a gut feeling of disgust.

People from all walks of life
are hooked on the fine white powder.
They use it to enhance their social
lives, or they use it at work,
supposedly to highlight their
performance. They go through their
days and evenings electrically
charged up. They spend their incomes
to feel superficially excited,
wonderful, and tingly all over.

Add
details   Slowly the drugged life becomes
their true reality and their real
life gets out of control. Everything
truly meaningful like homelife,
family, friends, relationships, and
self-worth, becomes secondary to the
dire need for cocaine. The more the
problems compile, such as late
bills, faltering relationships, and
hassles at work, the larger the need
to escape to the drug world.

My sister Sharon was one of
these people. By the time she was
twenty-one, she was married to a
cocaine dealer who was wanted in
Canada for dealing cocaine. He
abused her mentally and physically,
but she couldn't break away because
she was addicted. By the time my
parents had found out and put the
pressure on her to get out of that
environment, Sharon had moved in
with another cocaine dealer. He
never beat her, but she found out
after a while that he was involved in
pornography. He took pictures of
naked women in airplanes. While she
was living with this man she had a
serious accident. The car she had
parked in the driveway, on top of the
hill, started rolling down towards
the trailer they lived in. Being on
cocaine at the time and feeling the
superman effect that cocaine
sometimes gives, she tried to

*Good
details*

singlehandedly stop the car from
hitting the trailer.

Sharon spent four hours in
surgery, where they grafted an
artery into her thigh and did
extensive repairs on her right leg
and hip. She is lucky to have a leg
according to the two orthopedic
surgeons who worked on her. My
parents begged her to move home after
the accident, but she refused. It
wasn't until she lost her job of
eight years, because she took too
much medical leave, that she was at
the end of her rope and wanted to
change her life.

Sharon now lives at home with my
parents. She has broken all ties
with the people of her previous
lifestyle. She attends community
college and is looking for a medical
receptionist job. My sister has
told me that the most important
thing about her life is that she

feels she is finally in control. <u>My</u>

Write about this again.

<u>sister was lucky that her family was</u>

<u>persistent in their fight to get her</u>

<u>out of the drug life;</u> some people

aren't as lucky. It is easy for me to

see how others are now destroying

their lives with cocaine; I saw it

slowly killing my sister.

Anonymous

567 words

All of the examples of daily writing included in this chapter were actually written by people learning to write. They are included not because they are brilliant writing, but because they sound honest. Honest is never boring. You don't have to agree with the writer's opinions in order to find them interesting. Each person is unique. Each has something to say. Writing is a means for both finding and saying those somethings.

Why Bother Doing Daily Writings? The medical experts tell us that exercise is good for us. Many people like to play Frisbee. Most will never be great Frisbee players; most will never compete in a Frisbee tournament. But that doesn't mean they shouldn't play. The running, jumping, and sweating are enough justification for playing. People probably look silly when they trip over their own feet while running after a flying Frisbee. Many individuals don't play to be the best; they play to play, so looking silly doesn't matter.

Writing is like playing Frisbee. When you try to write just

what you mean and don't quite get it said, so what? You will do better the next time. You will make mistakes. You may even feel silly, but making mistakes and feeling silly are part of the learning process.

There are two excellent reasons for daily writing. The first is practice. The second is generating ideas for more writing, for writing essays. That is why it is important to keep track of the writing you do each day.

Keeping Track of Daily Writing Assignments

Experience suggests that four daily writing tasks per week is enough. In ten or fifteen minutes, a person can produce around two hundred words, maybe more. With practice, it is easy to write about a thousand words per week. At that rate, the writer will start seeing his or her work improve after about five weeks. The writer should count the words in each daily writing effort and then write the number of words on the top of the page. That way a person can see his or her writing speed increase. Use the "Daily Writing Record Sheet" to help you keep track of your word production.

DAILY WRITING RECORD SHEET

DAILY WRITING: The top of each daily writing effort should be labeled with the date, day of the week, and number of words. Note the number of words in the appropriate space below.

WEEK #	MONDAY	TUESDAY	WEDNESDAY	THURSDAY	FRIDAY
1.					
2.					
3.					
4.					
5.					
6.					
7.					
8.					
9.					
10.					

SPECIAL WRITING: Sometimes a person just feels like writing. When this happens, *do the writing.* Keep track of these efforts in the spaces provided below by noting topic, date, and number of words.

1. _____
2. _____
3. _____
4. _____
5. _____
6. _____
7. _____
8. _____
9. _____
10. _____
11. _____
12. _____
13. _____
14. _____
15. _____
16. _____
17. _____
18. _____
19. _____
20. _____

ACTIVITIES

A. *Working alone*

1. Do the daily writing assignments suggested in this chapter. Quantity, for now, is more important than quality, so write quickly and get as many words down on paper as you can. Use the "Daily Writing Record Sheet" to keep track of your word production.

2. About once a week, choose one of your daily writing efforts, and write on it two or three of the comments suggested in the "Responding to Daily Writing Assignments" section of this chapter. Any day's writing will do. Do you use enough examples and details? Can you find places to add some? Does your writing sound honest to you?

B. *Working with others*

1. Have someone else read your daily writing for the week and look for interesting or unusual ideas and opinions. These ideas and opinions might be good starting places for additional writing or for that week's "Rethink."

2. Exchange Thursday's "Rethinks" with someone, and write on them two or three of the comments suggested in the "Responding to Daily Writing Assignments" section of this chapter. Remember that these comments are *only* suggestions.

3. Each week, type your Thursday "Rethink" and hand it in to a teacher or other more experienced writer. Ask that person to write two or three of the comments suggested in the "Responding to Daily Writing Assignments" section of this chapter. Remember that this reader is not judging you but, rather, making suggestions about how you can improve your writing.

C. *Working with either small groups or by yourself*

1. Read the examples of daily writing included in this chapter, and put two response terms on each.

2. Read the examples of daily writing, and select opinions or ideas from them that you might choose for "Rethinks" if these were pieces you had written.
3. Write a "Rethink" starting with one of the ideas or opinions identified in Activity **C.2**. Remember to use specific details and examples to support your ideas and opinions.

Chapter

2

A WRITING PROCESS
Prewriting and Writing an Essay

Brain aerobics

Writing is a process. Professional writers don't just sit down and write articles. They get ready to write by collecting information —finding and reading other articles and books about the subject they are going to write about, interviewing experts, checking to see which magazines or publishers might buy what they will write, and thinking about issues relevant to their subjects. The work starts well before the professional writer starts writing the article itself. Most people call these getting-ready-to-write activities *prewriting.*

Next, most professional writers review the information they have gathered from their prewriting, and then they write a first or initial draft. Once a writer has a draft, he or she will most likely share it with someone else; the writer will get advice from one or more other people on how to make the draft better.

Normally, someone writing an article for a magazine or professional journal will write a draft, get suggestions from someone else on how to improve it, make changes to improve the draft based on those suggestions, share the new draft with someone who will make additional suggestions for improving the draft, make more changes in the draft to make it better, and so on. Many writers end up writing an article five to ten times before sending it to an editor who might or might not decide to publish it. Often the draft of an article will be returned by the editor with suggestions for additional improvements. Rarely does anyone get anything published that has only been written once. This is true of poems, short stories, essays, professional articles, novels, and other books. Writers, no matter what kinds of writing they do, go through a *process* of prewriting, writing, and then rewriting.

You need to write a paper, an essay. Since you will write several essays for this course, this one needs to be written in about a week. Yes, professional writers often spend months working on one essay. No, you will not have that luxury. There are deadlines in school and on the job. One does the best one can in the time available.

The important part of writing this first essay is the process —prewriting, writing, getting some suggestions from someone else, and then rewriting. Later in this book there will be more suggestions and exercises to help you be more thorough and efficient in each part of this process. For now, the job is to complete a short version of it.

Each person is different. Each writer develops, through time and through many drafts of many pieces of writing, his or her own writing process and writing style. This development requires time, energy, and effort, but most of all it requires practice. To be a writer, a person has to write. Some guidance in becoming a better and better writer speeds up the learning process. What follows is one way to move from a need to write to a good draft of an essay. There are many ways to do this, but the one presented here has helped many people many times. It is a good place to start.

PREWRITING: Creating a Focus

There is a difference between a *subject* for writing and an *issue* about which to write. A subject is very large, like U.S. Military Aid to the Third World, The Depression, or Federal Income Taxation Strategies; many books have been written on these subjects. People do not write essays on subjects; writers write essays on issues.

Issues are small parts of subjects. A subject might be the costs of higher education; an issue within this subject area might be "proposed increases in tuition for undergraduates on a particular campus." A subject might be physical fitness; an issue within this larger subject might be "the health benefits of walking for elderly citizens."

When preparing to write an essay, you need to choose an issue, but you need two more things. A writer needs a clear idea of at least one of his or her attitudes or opinions about that issue, and it is also helpful to have an initial idea of an intended audience. These three things together make what many people call the *focus* for an essay.

The subject for an essay is often assigned. Assigned subjects usually are those on which people have differing opinions. Environmental pollution, aging, and illiteracy in America are examples of such subjects. Nearly everyone has heard of and thought about these kinds of subjects. Better still, subjects like these are so large that most people most of the time have had some direct contact with them. This is a good place to start when looking for an issue that is part of an assigned subject. For example, say the assigned subject is aging. Everyone gets older day by day, so everyone knows something about that. Most people have friends and family members who are older than they are. On this and on most subjects, the writer can start with what he or she knows. One way to do this is to write down what you believe or remember about the subject, in this case aging. Write anything that comes to mind. This writing can be very much like the Monday daily writing assignment, "What I really think about . . . ," or it can be more like a brainstorming list. You are looking for the ways that your thoughts and your experiences relate to the assigned subject. An essay "says" something; you are looking for something to say.

Another useful strategy is thinking about what kinds of problems remain to be solved. Once again, if the subject is aging, ask yourself what kinds of problems older citizens face. What about transportation? What about nutrition? Are there problems with healthcare? Specific problems can be excellent issues about which to write.

A third strategy for discovering an issue about which to write, and one that is especially useful when preparing to write on an assigned subject, is to review your course notes. What facts or ideas in those notes are surprising or interesting? When possible, it is always wise to choose an issue that matters to you. There is no set formula for finding an issue. Writing down your ideas, thinking about problems, and reviewing course notes are things most writers do. They are good places to start. Once you have selected or discovered an issue, you can consider what your opinions about that issue are. People frequently know their own opinions about an issue as soon as they have decided to write about it. Just as often, however, people will take time at this stage not only to list their opinions but to think about why they have them. This is a good idea because you may find that you hold opinions you have never examined very closely. You may occasionally find that what you thought you thought is not what you think at all. A particular opinion may be what someone you respect told you to think, or it may be something you used to believe but now do not. Such a discovery is excellent because a newly discovered opinion adds interest and energy to a writing project.

The third part of a focus is an audience. It is not always necessary to have an audience in mind at this point, but it can help. Choosing an audience takes some thought. The choice of a specific audience depends on the issue and the writer's opinion concerning it. If the writer wants to change something, he or she might choose someone for the audience who can influence that change. One wouldn't, for example, write to a state patrolman if one were trying to change a traffic law. Such decisions are usually made by state legislators or by committees of state legislators.

The writer who wants to alert readers to a particular problem or opportunity would choose to write to someone who is likely to be interested in that problem or opportunity. A writer who wants to alert others to a summer softball program for twelve-year-olds, for example, might write to parents of twelve-year-olds.

Three qualifiers are needed here. First, the audience toward whom the writer starts out directing the essay might change *during the process.* Second, the audience that the writer has in mind may or may not ever see the essay the writer writes. Mostly, selecting an intended audience helps the writer clarify his or her own thinking. Third, naming an audience that includes many types of people is not very useful. Saying that the audience is the general public, for example, does not give the writer much to work with. On this first essay, your essay, identifying one particular person or one particular type of person is more helpful.

Once again, an issue, an opinion or an attitude toward that issue, and an intended audience add up to what many call a *focus* for an essay. Finding a focus is always part of prewriting for an essay.

The following are suggestions for subjects to start with. They are limited geographically to encourage you to draw upon your own background and experience.

Poverty in the community where you were raised
Crime in your present neighborhood
Illiteracy in the high school you attended
Some problem or annoyance connected to the campus on
   which you are studying

Here are some examples of focuses:

Subject: **Some problem or annoyance connected to the campus on which you are studying.**

Possible Issue	Writer's Opinion	Intended Audience
a. The bookstore is not open in the evening.	It should be.	The manager of the bookstore
b. The copy machines at the library don't work.	They should.	The Head Librarian
c. The dormitory rooms are too cold in the winter.	Students shouldn't have to freeze.	The Director of Student Services

1. Create a focus for an essay by (a) selecting an issue, (b) stating an attitude or an opinion about that issue, and (c) choosing an audience. (See Figure 2.1.) It is useful to write a brief description of your intended audience. What does this person look like? How is he or she dressed? What kinds of things does this person care about?
2. Share your focus, in small groups, with other students. Ask them for suggestions about how best to share your ideas about your issue with your intended audience.

Figure 2.1

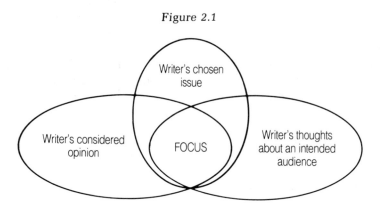

MORE PREWRITING: Writing to Write

There are many kinds of prewriting, some of which will be presented later in this book. For this essay, use only three in addition to the prewriting necessary to find a focus for the project. As a general rule, completing three prewriting activities for each writing project is a minimum. This allows the writer to look at a project from at least three different directions and furnishes him or her with more raw material.

1. The first of these three you have already practiced. Simply sit down and write what you really think about *your issue* for ten or fifteen minutes. Write hard and fast and don't worry about spelling or punctuation.
2. Next, think of what in your own experience suggested this issue to you. What got you thinking about this? Then describe in writing, for ten or fifteen minutes, the incident that caused or might have caused you to be concerned about this issue. For example, if you are prewriting about the copy machines in the library that are rarely operational, write a little story about what happened to you the last time you tried to use one of those machines. Include as many details as possible. If you can't think of such an incident, make one up.
3. The third prewriting activity for this essay project is making a list. You have a focus; you know your opinion on this issue. Now make a list of things people who don't agree with you might say about it. For example, if you are writing about why the bookstore should be open in the evening, those who disagree might say things like the following:
   a. "But nobody would use the bookstore after five p.m."
   b. "But increasing our business hours would increase our overhead, so we'd have to charge more for the books."
   c. "People who really need a book can arrange to come during the hours the bookstore is open."
   Anticipating what those who don't agree with you will say is part of your job. It is part of prewriting; it is part of being prepared. Making a list of possible objections can help you to clarify the focus for your essay. If you think about these objec-

tions and then write out your responses to them, you will have even more ideas to work with.

WRITING: Writing the First Draft

Having found a focus and having completed three kinds of prewriting, you are ready to write a draft.

First, you need to gather up all the prewriting you have done so far. Then you need to read it. Next, and this isn't easy, you should put all that prewriting away, out of sight, out of reach. Referring to your prewriting while writing tends to slow you down.

The time has come. You need to write the draft. On a personal computer or on paper, write the first or initial draft. Write quickly. Plan to keep writing for about forty minutes. *Do not worry.* Do not worry about spelling or punctuation. Do not worry about grades; this is only the first draft. You will have time to make improvements on it later. At this point, just write and keep writing. You want to produce a whole draft with a beginning, middle, and end. After you have written it, you might consider typing it. This makes the next step easier. If you draft on a personal computer or typewriter, you will already have a typed copy.

REWRITING: Improving Your Draft

Once you have a draft, it is wise to get ideas for improving it from someone else. Trade drafts with someone in your class or small group. Each of you then reads the other's paper and writes *only some* of the following comments on it:

1. Add an example here.
2. Good example.
3. Add details here.
4. Good details.
5. Write more about this.
6. This sounds honest.
7. This part might be left out.
8. You've lost me.

Use only these eight comments, and don't use them all. Three or four comments on a draft are more helpful than ten or twenty. As writer, remember that these are only suggestions. As the reader of someone else's draft, remember to suggest improvements. Just writing *"Good example"* on a draft three times might make the writer feel good, but it doesn't help that writer think about how to improve the draft.

If possible, put your draft with someone else's suggestions on it away for twenty-four hours and don't worry about it. After twenty-four hours, reread all your prewriting and the suggestions someone else has written on your draft. Then read your draft. Using a personal computer, or scissors and tape if you don't have a PC, add details and examples to your draft. If you like, take out sentences or paragraphs that don't seem to belong in the draft. Make those changes you feel will make your draft better.

Once you have made these changes, type a copy of your latest draft. Most teachers and all employers expect you to type the writing you submit to them. It is part of your job.

For this draft (the typed draft), you should look up the spelling of words you use but are not sure how to spell. You should also use the best punctuation you can.

After you have typed your draft, read it again and fix, in pencil, any typing or spelling mistakes you find. Next have someone else read your paper looking for such mistakes, and then fix the mistakes that person finds.

The essay is now ready to be turned in to the instructor. It may not be perfect, but it is probably good. Better still, if you have done your best at every stage of the process — prewriting, writing, and rewriting — then both you and your instructor will know better which parts of the process you need to practice more. The rest of this book is designed to help you get the understanding and the practice you need to be a better and better writer at each stage of the writing process.

Chapter 3

THINKING ABOUT THE VARIABLES

A Communication Situation Model

© 1985 Universal Press Syndicate

"Hey! I think you've hit on
something there! Sheep's clothing!
Sheep's clothing! . . . Let's get out of
these gorilla suits!"

Whenever a person shares thoughts and experiences with someone else, that person is communicating. Communicating is something people are very good at. Some experts write that people need to communicate just as much as they need to eat and sleep. This is probably true. If you are ever around children, you know that most of them make plenty of noise; they seem to enjoy making noise. Sometimes it seems like all they are saying is "look at me," but they *are* communicating. As children grow up, they learn to organize their noise into words and sentences. Later, they learn to adjust what they say to meet the needs of the person they are saying it to, and they figure out that there are things they should not say in certain situations. There are, for example, certain issues that are not discussed at the dinner table.

Through time, each person becomes a better and better communicator. This happens naturally. People communicate in many ways, but the two main ways are speaking and writing. Each person practices speaking every day. Writing is a different matter, yet speaking and writing are very similar. Both are tools for communication.

THINKING ABOUT COMMUNICATION

Over two thousand years ago, Aristotle studied communication. He called the study of communication *rhetoric*. He defined rhetoric as "finding or discovering (and utilizing) in *a given situation* the available means of persuasion." People want to persuade others to do or consider something new; they want to communicate. As they search their minds and experience for appropriate resources, for "the available means of persuasion," they consider the factors involved; (1) the issue or issues in question; (2) the effects that these communication efforts will have if successful (purpose); (3) the knowledge, experience, and opinions of the readers or listeners (the audience); and (4) the way they wish to be perceived by the audience.

These four factors, at least, are aspects of any conscious act of communication. Another definition of rhetoric, then, is "an applied theory of communication." Very simply, one can plan ahead how best to communicate. Communication is often represented by the triangle in Figure 3.1.

An important additional factor—especially in spoken

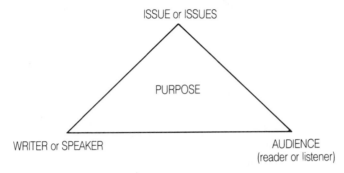

Figure 3.1

communication — is what might best be called *timing*. Taken all together then, there are at least five factors to consider in a communication or rhetorical situation, although timing is not always something a writer can control.

Thinking About the Variables in Spoken Communication

Think about this for a minute. Years ago a student needed a part-time job, and his friend was working for a restaurant that needed another waiter. The friend took the student to a men's clothing store and helped him choose a shirt, tie, and slacks. The shirt was white, the tie blue, and the slacks gray (all the waiters at this restaurant wore white shirts and gray slacks). The friend lent the student the money for these purchases.

He then told the student that the boss was a retired Marine and liked short hair and to be called "Sir." He also told him that this restaurant had many customers from 11:00 a.m. to 1:30 p.m. and from 5:30 p.m. to 10:00 p.m. each day.

So the student got a haircut and went to meet the boss about 4:00 p.m. when things were quiet, and he went dressed for the job. He responded to the potential employer's questions with "Yes, Sir," or "No, Sir" and got the job. In part, the timing (when the boss wasn't busy), the clothes (just what the boss expected),

ISSUE:
The job of waiting on tables.

PURPOSE:
Gainful employment.

SPEAKER or WRITER:
The student with short hair,
dressed like a waiter,
being respectful.

AUDIENCE:
The one-time Marine
who worked long hours
and expected respect
from his employees.

Timing: When the boss was not busy.

Figure 3.2

the haircut, and the word "Sir" got the student the job. It was not a great job, but it let the student start eating more regularly and start making a living. The point is that he went prepared; he did his "prewriting." Look at the communication situation triangle in Figure 3.2.

This student, with the help of his very good friend, got the job waiting tables. He went to ask the boss for the job *after* he had thought about the variables in the communication situation.

1. The *issue* was obvious — the job of waiting tables.
2. The speaker's *purpose* was also clear — getting the job.
3. In this situation, the most important factor was the *audience*. By talking to his friend, the student learned the following about his intended audience:
   a. The boss was an ex-Marine.
      (1) He liked to be called "Sir."
      (2) He didn't like to see long hair on the heads of males who worked for him.
      (3) He wanted his waiters to wear white shirts, gray slacks, and ties.

   b. The boss was busy doing *his* job from 11:00 a.m. to 1:30 p.m.
      and from 5:30 p.m. to 10:00 p.m. each day.
4. Adding this information up, the student decided to present
   himself as the kind of person the boss wanted to hire.
   a. He got the "right" haircut.
   b. He called the boss "Sir."
   c. He went to ask for work already dressed for the job.
5. The *timing* was important to this communication situation.
   The student knew when the boss would be free to talk with
   him and timed his visit accordingly.

   In this example, rhetoric was used in obvious and practical
ways to help the student achieve an obvious and practical end —
getting a job. But rhetoric can do much more. Rhetoric can help
people figure out what they really think and feel. Rhetoric can
help people *discover* truths about situations and about themselves.

Thinking About the Variables in
Written Communication

   So what does all this have to do with writing? Quite a bit in
fact. In writing you get to choose how you present yourself. What
you say in writing and how you say it create an image of you in
the mind of a reader. In the previous section, the student presented himself (the clothes and haircut) so he looked like the type
of person that the boss wanted to have working for him. The
same can be done in writing.
   Consider this communication situation. A person who has
planned to go camping with friends in April receives an invita-
tion to her grandparents' fiftieth wedding anniversary celebra-
tion, which is scheduled for the same weekend as the camping
trip. She has already paid for her part of the camping trip and
does not feel she can back out. She decides to write a letter
explaining her decision not to attend the anniversary party. What
follows are two different approaches to this letter.
   In the first approach, the writer simply wants to get the
letter in the mail. She sits down and quickly writes whatever

comes into her head. She is only thinking of herself, of how inconvenient it is for her to have to write the letter. Predictably, the letter looks like this:

Dear Grandpa and Grandma:
    I'm sorry I can't come to your party. I've already made other plans. Fifty years is a long time. Kind of scary to think about. Anyway, I hope it's lots of fun and, again, sorry I can't make it.

Love,
Judy

The second approach is to think a little before writing; see the communication situation triangle in Figure 3.3.

Figure 3.3

The resulting letter is significantly different from the first:

Dear Gramps and Grannie,
    I was surprised to hear that your anniversary celebration was so close. It sounds as if everyone has gone to a great deal of effort and planning to make this a special and memorable occasion, and I'm sure all will appreciate it and have a wonderful time.

        I wish I could be there to join in the festivities,
but I'm committed to other plans for the same weekend,
unfortunately. Four of us have planned a camping trip for
spring break, and we've paid a non-refundable deposit on
the cabin. So, as you can see, I'm obligated to follow
through on my commitments. And, as Grandpa always taught
me, a person must keep his word.
        Please accept my congratulations. I will come to
visit in June and show you the pictures of the camping trip
if you'll show me the photos from the party.

                                                        Love,
                                                        Judy

    On one level, the point here is simple; by taking a little extra
planning time, Judy has made her grandparents feel better and
herself look good. She has considered other people's feelings as
well as her own. She is using good rhetoric; she is thinking ahead
about the variables.

    She is also accomplishing much more. She starts out with a
fairly simple purpose — gracefully explaining why she can't attend the party. After thinking about it, however, she realizes that
a fiftieth wedding anniversary is scary not only to her but to her
grandparents as well. Therefore her second letter emphasizes the
connections between her and her grandparents, and in that letter
she makes another commitment. She promises to share time and
memories with these two important participants in her life. Rhetoric has helped Judy to clarify not only her thinking but her
feelings. She has used rhetoric to help her discover something
about herself.

Thinking Again About the Variables in Written Communication

    Imagine a student in a writing class who has been asked to
write about stress. Since she has been using this book, she already has two or three weeks' worth of daily writing assignments.
As prewriting, she decides to sit down and write "What I really
think about stress."

''What I really think about stress''

I often think I'm the expert on pressure--I'm the one
who's ''stressed-out'' all the time, but then I see other
people--whose problems seem pretty silly to me--their
cats are sick or the fuel pump in their Volvo is broken,
and I think--boy that person has it easy--kill the stupid
cat, fix the Volvo, and get on with it.

But over the last few years I've decided two things.
One, each person feels their problems are the world's
worst, <u>and</u>, whatever kinds of problems--money, school,
relationships--the ones a person is facing <u>right then</u> are
the worst anyone could ever face.

For example, when I was in high school, I had a heavy
load at school, a little sister my mother wanted me to
raise, essay exams, a job nights that payed minimum wage,
<u>and</u> I was too young to face all those things. So, I
thought my stress, my problems, were bigger than
anyone's--and the worst I'd ever faced. Three years
later, I've still got problems--about as many--and this
set seems pretty bad.

Anonymous
277 words

Next, the student reads this over looking for an issue or an
opinion to write about. She sees several opinions in it already,
and she thinks of other ideas while reading it.

One opinion already expressed is that people always seem
to feel stress. It seems as though no matter how life is going,
people always have things to worry about. Her opinion is that
feeling stress is part of being human.

Another opinion in that short piece of writing is that present
problems often seem worse than problems one has faced in the
past. Problems are like nightmares, she thinks. When she's having one, it seems pretty terrible. When she thinks about it later, it
doesn't seem so bad. This other idea, then, is that it's very hard to
see problems in perspective when a person is in the middle of
them.

Thinking about it now, it seems strange to the writer that she would worry about worrying—that she would feel stress about stress. She has read that stress causes health problems and that when a person has a health problem, stress can make it worse. Maybe a third idea, then, is that problems cause other problems, that stress causes stress.

Now that she has got some ideas to start with, it is time to think about the variables. It sometimes works best when one considers audience next. Who would benefit from reading what she has to write about stress? Who would be interested?

A few words of caution here. Some people think the only possible audience for an assigned essay is the person who made the assignment, the teacher. This is generally not true. Teachers know that most students are pretty good at guessing what the teacher wants to read and then writing that. On an essay test, this is a good idea; otherwise, it probably is not. Remember that an essay presents the *writer's* opinions or ideas and the thinking behind them. Most teachers would rather read your opinions and your ideas than your attempts to guess at theirs. Therefore, rather than thinking the teacher is the audience, think of someone else. Your audience should be a single person to start with, not a huge class of people.

Returning now to this essay about stress, who could the audience be? Let's look at some possibilities. If the student writes about her first opinion—that experiencing stress is part of being human—she might choose someone she knows who hasn't experienced enough stress yet to know that it is just part of living, that it is unavoidable.

Just to look at the variables, then, she considers writing to her fifteen-year-old niece. This niece is smart and pretty, and her parents have always provided for both her needs and her wants. Fifteen years is, as this writer remembers, a very stressful age. At fifteen, a person is learning about working, wondering about sexuality, and struggling with his or her own emotions.

Looking at the communication situation triangle in Figure 3.4 (page 50), this writer can see that such an essay probably won't work. Thinking about it, she can't come up with a way to present herself as writer so that this audience will "hear" what

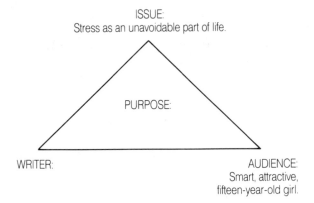

Figure 3.4

she has to say. This fifteen-year-old, and fifteen-year-olds in general, don't pay much attention to what adults say. The other problem is purpose; what could her essay hope to achieve? It would not be good to tell this adolescent, "Sure you're feeling a lot of stress now, but get used to it — it gets worse." No, this is not an essay she could write. Maybe when her niece is a little older, this writer will give it a try. Maybe not.

The second opinion this writer discovered in her short writing effort is that present problems always seem worse than problems faced in the past. Who could she write to about that? She has a friend named Jim. He is her age (early twenties), has a college education, and is unemployed. Jim and she hike, cook, fish, and work on cars together. They are friends. She knows him pretty well, and right now, because he is unemployed, he is what they call "stressed-out." She prepares a triangle (Figure 3.5) to look at the variables for the communication situation of her writing to Jim about stress.

Because she is thinking about someone she knows instead of a big category of people (such as all unemployed people), she knows what to think about next. She needs to consider how to present herself as writer so that Jim will be receptive to what she has to say. If she tried to present herself as some big expert on stress, Jim would not read past the first paragraph of her essay; he

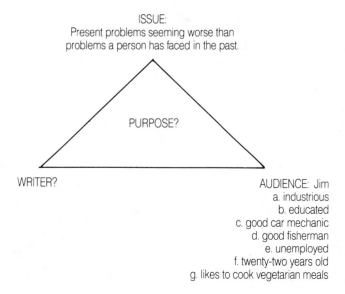

Figure 3.5

wouldn't want her telling him what to do. So maybe she should present herself as someone who has been unemployed before, who knows something about what Jim is feeling right then, and who thinks he is strong enough, talented enough, and industrious enough to put up with the stress he is feeling and get on with his life. Her purpose then becomes one of praising and reassuring Jim; he needs, in her opinion, the emotional support.

This writer feels good about her revised communication situation triangle (see Figure 3.6, p. 52); now she has a focus. She could write this essay. However, as reader, you might be thinking, "Sure, she is going to write a letter to her friend; it won't be an essay at all."

If you think that, you are only partially correct. The writer is not going to write directly to Jim. She is going to write an essay, keeping Jim in mind while she writes. This is an old technique but a good one.

Remember that writing is a form of communication and that it takes at least two people, a writer and a reader, for written

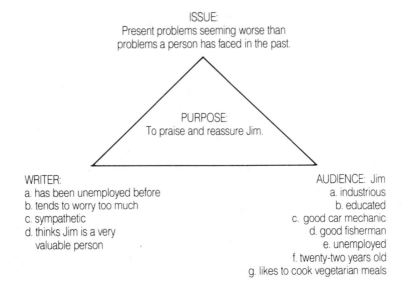

ISSUE:
Present problems seeming worse than
problems a person has faced in the past.

PURPOSE:
To praise and reassure Jim.

WRITER:
a. has been unemployed before
b. tends to worry too much
c. sympathetic
d. thinks Jim is a very
   valuable person

AUDIENCE: Jim
a. industrious
b. educated
c. good car mechanic
d. good fisherman
e. unemployed
f. twenty-two years old
g. likes to cook vegetarian meals

Figure 3.6   •

communication to take place. Imagining that you are writing to *a person who would be interested in what you have to say* is very important. It makes it easier to write.

There is another advantage to using this technique. When you think of a *real* person as your audience when writing, what you write is more understandable to other *real* readers. This imaginary writer can tell herself she is writing to people who are in Jim's situation—twenty-two years old, educated, unemployed, and "stressed-out." They will have some of the same concerns, attitudes, and feelings that Jim has. She can write to them by imagining herself writing to him.

You will need to practice this technique several times before it will work for you, so give it a chance. In fact, give it about ten chances before you decide whether it works for you. It is a very good technique for preparing to write, for prewriting. Basically, by imagining a real person as audience a writer can produce an essay that is understandable to real readers.

CONSIDERING THE VARIABLES
IN COMMUNICATION SITUATIONS:
Why Practice Rhetoric?

The key in any communication situation is thinking about your opinions and ideas about an issue, analyzing the audience that needs to hear what you have to say, considering how best to present yourself to that audience, and identifying the purpose you hope to achieve with the writing. The key is being prepared.

If you still are not convinced that using rhetoric is a good idea, then remember the reasons that Aristotle gave for learning to think about communication situations. Aristotle, who some call the "father of rhetoric," had his own answers to the question, "Why bother to learn rhetoric?" He named four ways that the art of rhetoric was valuable:

1. When used well by a good person, rhetoric can prevent the triumph of fraud and injustice. It is not enough just to have good intentions. Those intentions must be powerfully and persuasively presented.
2. Rhetoric helps people to persuade or instruct when scientific proofs and arguments are not enough. Science, although a powerful tool, is not relevant to many issues. What does science tell us about right and wrong, for example?
3. Rhetoric teaches us to see both sides of an issue. Each person knows what he or she believes, but that person should also consider what people think who don't agree.
4. Rhetoric helps people to defend themselves with words. Aristotle was aware that each person has interests to look after. He also knew that a person didn't have to be honest to be persuasive, so everybody needed to know the tools of persuasion.

There are other reasons to study and practice rhetoric. The conscious use of rhetorical principles — thinking communication situations through ahead of time — gives a person power. Like Aristotle, most people think it's a shame when a good idea is lost because it is not well presented. Most people also believe that, given the opportunity, people will choose to do what is good rather than what is bad.

Did you ever think back on a conversation or on something you have written and say to yourself, "What I should have said (or written) was . . . ." After the communication has happened, it is too late to prepare for it. Thinking about a communication situation *before it happens* improves the quality of the communication both in writing and speaking.

As the preceding examples have shown, the important parts of any communication situation triangle are not necessarily the corners. Finding an issue, an audience, and a purpose is just the beginning. Far more important are the connections between writer and issue, issue and audience, and writer and audience; see Figure 3.7.

Aristotle presented rhetoric primarily as a tool for persuasion, but he also saw it as a way for people to recall what they already knew about an issue *and* as a means through which they could discover new ideas and opinions. In this way, rhetoric is a tool for discovering new thoughts. More than an aid to effective communication, rhetoric is a tool that people can use to improve their understanding of issues, of others, and of themselves.

Figure 3.7

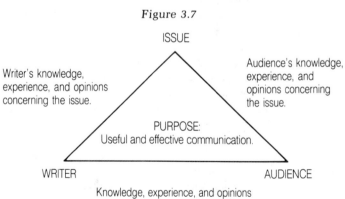

ISSUE

Writer's knowledge, experience, and opinions concerning the issue.

Audience's knowledge, experience, and opinions concerning the issue.

PURPOSE: Useful and effective communication.

WRITER

AUDIENCE

Knowledge, experience, and opinions concerning the issue that the writer and audience share and opinions that they do not share.

ACTIVITIES

A. *Working alone*
1. Write a version of the student's conversation with his potential employer (pages 43–45). Remember that when writing dialogue, the writer must start a new paragraph each time the speaker changes.
2. Select a communication situation from your own experience or imagination, and write out your thoughts about
   a. issue
   b. purpose (desired effect or result)
   c. audience
   d. how to present yourself
   e. timing
3. Repeat Activity A.2 three or four times.

B. *Working with others*
1. Share your versions of the conversation in Activity **A.1**. Which conversations are most likely to achieve the student's purpose? Why?
2. With other people in your small group or with the whole class, discuss the ethics of the student getting the job (pages 43–45). The student got his hair cut; was he being dishonest? The student went to the job interview prepared; was he manipulating the boss?
3. Discuss why the author of this chapter might think that all communication involves rhetoric? Is that generalization true? How is it true?
4. Over two thousand years ago, Aristotle gave the four reasons for studying rhetoric mentioned in this chapter. Are these still good reasons? Use examples of communication situations to argue for or against Aristotle's four reasons.

C. *Suggestions for another writing project*
1. Read all of your Wednesday daily writing ("Responding to something you have read"), and choose one of the issues or opinions about which you have written.

2. Start with this issue or opinion; then think about your issue, purpose, audience, and how to present yourself, and make a communication situation triangle.
3. Write a two-page first draft of an essay based on your communication situation triangle.
4. Exchange drafts with someone in your class, and make some of the suggestions for improving the drafts presented in the "Rewriting" section of Chapter 2.
5. Using some of these suggestions, rewrite your essay draft.

Chapter 4

SOMETHING TO SAY
Preparing to Write

© 1984 Universal Press Syndicate

The Vikings, of course, knew the importance of stretching before an attack.

Sometimes people, and especially students, are given subjects to write about. Certainly part of an education is thinking, speaking, and writing about current problems in the world in which we live. Students are asked to write about terrorism, law enforcement, computers, state taxes, and other subjects discussed in the newspapers and on the six o'clock TV news. One problem with such subjects is that if they really are current, then everyone is thinking, speaking, and writing about them. Educators tend to ask students to develop new perspectives on these subjects, and here again we face a problem of rhetoric.

Think for a minute about high-school and college writing teachers. Most have taught writing for several years and have read thousands of student essays. Most teachers also read many newspaper and news magazine articles, professional journals, and books, and almost all have been avid readers for years. So the writing student is in a bind. First, a particular teacher (who may be the only audience) might know more about a subject than the student. Second, the teacher may have already seen hundreds of student essays about terrorism, law enforcement, computers, state taxes, or whatever. So how does the student come up with something new to say?

Students are not the only people who need to come up with new perspectives and ideas. Each of us is expected to have opinions on important and unimportant subjects and issues; each of us needs to have things to say. Our culture values the individual and each individual's contributions and opinions. It encourages independent thought. Fortunately, each individual's unique experience and perspective can provide resources for new insights or the enrichment of widely shared opinions or beliefs.

The following are strategies for finding (discovering or remembering) these new ideas or perspectives to talk and write about, for prewriting. They are also useful for writers who know what they want to write about but who need to find and develop examples, details, facts, and arguments that will support their perspectives and make them understandable to real readers. Nobody would use every one of them every time he or she prepares to write an essay, but each strategy will be useful some of the time. All of these strategies can help when an instructor assigns a broad subject for an essay and asks students to choose their own narrower issues from within it.

MORE PREWRITING STRATEGIES

Writing as a Way to Remember or Discover

One of the best ways to find things to write about is to write. Since you have been doing daily writing assignments, you have already practiced this. Your daily writing notebook is, in part, a resource book for issues, ideas, opinions, and perspectives. Another important part of daily writing is getting into the *habit* of writing. People get good at doing things they do regularly. Once you are in the habit of writing, it becomes easier.

In Chapter 3, the woman who was writing about stress couldn't find any writing in her notebook about stress, so she just sat down and wrote for ten or fifteen minutes about it. This is a very good idea. In this phase of prewriting, spelling and grammar do not count; the writer is usually the only person who ever reads it, so just getting the ideas down is important. Writing whatever comes into your mind about an assigned essay subject for ten or fifteen minutes three or more times is smart. You will be creating a storehouse of ideas and issues, a written record of your own perspectives. Reading this writing later, you might find clues that will help you to identify an issue, opinion, and audience for your essay.

Writing a Narrative (Story)

One of the ways to approach an issue or subject is to write about an incident from the writer's past experience. This could be something that really happened, or the author could imagine or make up the incident.

Say, for example, that you were asked to write about consumer debt. Did you ever buy something on credit and then have trouble making the payments? You could certainly write about that. Perhaps someone you know has gotten into a serious debt situation. You could write about that problem. Even if neither you nor anyone you know has experienced consumer-debt difficulties, it is fairly easy to imagine how such things can happen.

Whether you are presenting events that happened or making them up, be sure to include specific details. Rather than "John had huge payments to make on his new car," write "John had to make payments of $348.50 each month on his new, candy-apple red, Chrysler Marquis." This kind of narrative gives readers an extended example.

Writing a brief narrative about an issue or subject is, for many people, one of the easiest ways to get started.

Reading for Ideas

No matter what subject you choose or are asked to write about, many other people have already written about it. Much of this writing is published. Libraries collect, catalogue, and store this material. When you are asked to write about a subject you know little or nothing about, the library can be your first stop. Better still, libraries employ people who will help you find what you are looking for. By paying close attention to what these people do and say, you can become very good at finding what you need without their help. Like learning to write by writing, you learn to use libraries by using them.

This is not a book about how to use libraries, but the following paragraphs contain helpful suggestions about using the books and articles you find in them. Many believe that articles in magazines, newspapers, and professional journals are the best resources for writers. They are easily found and quickly read. They often contain the very latest facts, opinions, and attitudes about their subjects. Just as important, they are usually essays, and people who write essays should read many essays written by others.

It is a good idea to keep track of what you are reading. Part of keeping track is being able to find the article again if you need to. You do this by noting down (1) the *author's name*; (2) the *title of the article*; (3) the *title of the magazine, newspaper, or journal* that contains it; (4) *the publication date* of that magazine, newspaper, or journal; and (5) *the numbers of the pages* on which the article appears. With this much information, you or anyone else could find the article again.

Most people already know how to copy out, word for word, interesting facts, opinions, and ideas that they find in other people's writing. These words should have quotation marks at both ends of them. The marks remind the notetaker that these words are someone else's, that they belong to the person who wrote them. Since you are quoting another author, these notes are called *quotations*.

A second kind of note is called a *paraphrase*. When you write down what the article's author is saying, but you write it in your own words, you are paraphrasing. Those ideas still belong to that other author, but you do not put quotation marks around them in your notes.

When you use these first two kinds of notes, direct quotations and paraphrases, in your own essays, you need to give credit to the author. It is dishonest to take someone else's words or ideas and present them as your own; it is also illegal. When you are reading for ideas, don't worry about breaking the law. Simply use quotation marks when you copy an author's sentences out word for word, and don't use quotation marks when you paraphrase.

Now, what about what *you think* while you are reading someone else's article? Your ideas while you are reading are the most important of all. *Write them down.* An old trick is to put [your ideas] in square brackets in your notes. That way you know what is what in your notes even if you took those notes days, weeks, or years in the past. For some reason, reading other people's ideas makes you have more of your own. This is why reading is such a powerful prewriting strategy.

Your notes, then, taken while reading an article, should look something like this:

Author's name. "Title of Article." *Title of magazine, newspaper, or journal*, date of publication. Page numbers.

(*page number*) "Sentences copied word for word from the article."

(*page number*) Paraphrases of facts, ideas, attitudes, or perspectives presented in the article.
[Within square brackets, the ideas, opinions, and facts that *you* think of while reading the article.]

When reading for ideas on any subject or issue, it is wise to read several different articles. It is better if these articles come from different types of publications. For example, if you are reading about current problems in public education, don't choose to read three articles in *Newsweek*. An article from *Newsweek*, another from your local newspaper, and a third from a journal written for and by educators would be better. Remember that you are looking for a variety of facts, ideas, and perspectives. Remember too that the most important words in your notes are those between square brackets — [the ideas *you* get while reading].

Talking as a Way to Prepare to Write

Another excellent prewriting strategy is talking. Each person is unique. Each person's experience is different. Talk to people. As with reading, variety is important here. It often seems that the older a person is, the more experience and ideas that person has. Older people are among the best resources for ideas and perspectives; they have done and seen so much. Younger people are valuable resources because they seem to question everything. Questions that have no fixed answers are often starting places for essays.

It is obvious, but choosing to speak with people who have special knowledge about a subject is wise. A person preparing to write about college athletics might talk to a football coach, a first baseman on the college team, and a sports reporter for the college newspaper. People enjoy talking about subjects about which they are experts.

The writer must remember that he or she is looking for information, opinions, and ideas — *not* for an argument. Save your arguments for your essays. Listening is the best part of talking about something. You may already know what you think, and what you think may change as you gather additional information.

Sometimes you can take notes while talking to someone. The strategies for taking notes are similar to those suggested for taking notes while reading. When talking to an expert, you can start your notes with the person's name, his or her title (for example, football coach for Western University, linebacker for Lincoln High School, store manager for the South Hill Safeway), and the date of the conversation. After that, the notes look about the same as the notes you take while reading:

"What the person said, word for word."
Your paraphrase of what the person said.
[What you said or thought while talking to the person.]

Don't just talk to experts. Everyone has valuable ideas and perspectives. What the other person says is important, and there are a few things you can say to help you better understand what that person is saying to you:

1. When you think you understand a point but are not quite sure, you can ask, "Could you give me an example?" Examples almost always increase understanding.
2. Another way to clarify a point is to paraphrase — to try to put what the other person is saying into your own words. Your question would start something like, "Do you mean . . . ?" This way, you will know if you have understood; if you have not, then the other person can help you out.
3. When the other person barely mentions something of interest to you, you can always ask, "Could you expand on that?" This other person has no way of knowing what does or does not interest you. Help that other person give you what you need.

Obviously, there are other valuable questioning strategies, but these three are very useful; they increase communication. By practicing them, you can become an even better communicator.

Identifying and Coining Oxymorons

Another prewriting strategy that can help a writer come up with a new angle or perspective is finding or creating oxymorons. An *oxymoron* is coined when two words that normally would seem to contradict one another are joined. For example, consider the term "fortunate mistake." We usually think of mistakes as having negative consequences. If you bake a chicken for an hour at 425 degrees rather than at 325 degrees, you are probably making a mistake. But not all mistakes are harmful. If a recipe calls for three cloves of garlic and you use six, you might make a tastier dish. To talk about these kinds of errors we need a term, and "fortunate mistake" works well. "Fortunate mistake" is an oxymoron, because people do not normally think of mistakes as fortunate.

Whether a term is an oxymoron or not depends on how you look at it. For one person, "economy car" might seem like an oxymoron. A car, any car, is expensive to buy, maintain, buy fuel for, and insure. Another person might say that "economy car" is not an oxymoron. Both people are correct; oxymorons are largely matters of perspective.

There are two ways that oxymorons can be used by someone looking for new perspectives to write about. First, a person can learn to recognize that some of the accepted terms that we hear everyday can be seen as oxymorons. A popular example of this is the term "military intelligence." Although this term is commonly used to refer to organizations that gather information about foreign military strength and activities, such as the Central Intelligence Agency, some people think that nothing the military does shows much intelligence. A student asked to write about American foreign policy might write about this oxymoron as part of his or her prewriting.

In the 1980s, the term "casual sex" became popular. For most people, sex is not something one participates in casually. Therefore, some people might think "casual sex" is an oxymoron. The term "casual sex" itself might be a good issue about which to write.

By watching for oxymorons in things people say and in what

you read, you can get better at spotting them. Oxymorons are, in a sense, matters of perspective. The expression "casual sex" might not look like an oxymoron to someone else, which is why learning to spot oxymorons is a valuable writing strategy. It encourages thinking about common expressions in uncommon ways.

Here is another example. Imagine a student who has been asked to write an essay about nutrition. She is in a nutrition course and has been reading about the harmful effects of caffeine, cholesterol, and processed sugar. As a prewriting strategy, she decides to go to a grocery store and look for oxymorons on product labels. Because she knows that sugar contributes to such medical problems as acne, diabetes, and heart disease, the expression "pure sugar" seems like an oxymoron. Other products provide food for thought. What, for example, is a "chocolate-chip health bar?" When she sees "diet ice cream," she nearly laughs out loud. Can people really lose weight by eating ice cream? This student carefully writes down the ingredients of some of these products. She may write for or against such products, may see them as positive or negative, or she may write an essay with some other opinion in mind. Whatever the slant, by starting with a new angle, she is starting well.

The other way to use oxymorons as a prewriting strategy is to make them up. This is difficult but not too difficult. You are playing with words.

Perhaps the easiest way to make up an oxymoron is to place a word next to its opposite, then think about what your new oxymoron might mean. Happy and sad are opposites. Is there such a thing as a "happy sadness?" What would a "peaceful war" be? A person preparing to write about law enforcement might coin the oxymoron "criminal law enforcement" or "illegal law enforcement." Someone thinking about the problems faced by senior citizens might consider fortunate older people who have financial security, health, and leisure time and call them the "young elderly."

Making or finding oxymorons is a thinking strategy; like any other thinking strategy, it will only be helpful part of the time. Once you have found or made an interesting oxymoron, write about it for ten minutes. Why is it an oxymoron? What do you think your oxymoron means?

Adopting a Persona

Another way to find fresh perspective on a subject or issue that has been widely discussed is to pretend that you, as speaker or writer, are someone else. There are at least two easy ways to do this. The first is to imagine yourself as someone more centrally concerned in the issues about which you are thinking or writing. Imagine what a terrorist would say about terrorism, for example, or what a state patrol officer would say about police brutality, and then write from that perspective.

A second way of adopting a persona is to determine how you really feel about an issue and then argue the opposite. If you feel that state taxes are too high, then argue that they should be higher. If you feel that computer skills will be necessary for success in any career, then argue that people should not use computers at all. This prewriting strategy is especially helpful when you feel, as everyone does from time to time, that you have nothing to say about an issue or subject.

When you think of yourself as someone more closely involved in an issue, as someone you are not, you might feel more free to play with ideas. Where does a state patrolman or patrolwoman spend the day? In an automobile on the freeway. How do the people with whom that person interacts treat him or her? Some are very respectful and some are hostile. What would it feel like if someone you didn't know acted like he hated you? Adopting a persona makes you put on another person's shoes and tie up the laces.

Writing the opposite of what you really think also gives you some added freedom. For many people, it is easier to write what they don't believe than to express what they actually think and feel. Writing the opposite of what you believe also helps you to see the perspectives of people with whom you disagree. Knowing what you think is important; knowing what people who don't agree with you believe is useful — especially to a writer.

Compare and Contrast

A thinking strategy people use all the time is *compare and contrast*. Whenever individuals are presented with choices, they instinctively begin to compare and contrast the traits of the alternatives in order to decide which is better for them. For example, a person about to buy a car might compare and contrast the prices, options, repair records, and estimated miles per gallon of gasoline ratings of several different cars.

Such thinking is easy to do and can be helpful when trying to find something different to speak or write about. One suggestion is not to choose two things to compare that seem very much alike. Don't, for example, compare prison and school—both have buildings, grounds, supervisors, and rules. Don't compare running shoes and dress shoes. Instead, when looking at two seemingly similar things—prisons and schools, for example—think mostly about the differences between them: not how they compare but how they contrast. Students do not stay in the same buildings twenty-four hours a day and 365 days a year; prisoners do.

Another way to use this kind of thinking is to make one of the things you choose to compare something related to the subject or issue about which you are preparing to write. If you are writing about education, for example, you might choose math exams. Then compare math exams with something *completely unrelated* to education. Compare things that are radically different. Compare a brother and a pocket comb, or a running shoe and a Boeing 747, or a math exam and a fish. How is terrorism like a baseball bat? How is NASA like a fire hydrant? One doesn't discover new perspectives by thinking about things in old and familiar ways.

Cause and Effect

Cause and effect thinking is one of the most common and most useful tools people have. When something happens, people want to know why, want to know what caused this something to happen. For example, when an airplane crashes, everyone wants to know the cause of the crash. Was it pilot error? Was the airplane properly maintained? Did a bird fly into an engine? It is generally believed that knowing the causes of a crash can help us to avoid other such tragedies.

Also, the crash itself becomes a cause that has effects. If the investigation following the crash reveals that a certain electronic system in the aircraft has malfunctioned, efforts would then be made to check other aircraft of the same model for such defects.

Thinking about causes and effects can be a very valuable prewriting strategy. It is easy to do, and this type of thinking can be as useful to the student who is trying to find an essay issue to write about as it is to the student who has already found one.

Imagine that an instructor has asked a student to write an essay about illiteracy. As part of the prewriting for this essay, the student thinks about causes and effects of illiteracy in the following ways:

1. First the student makes a list of every cause of illiteracy that he or she can think of.

Causes of Illiteracy

no education	TV
poverty	drug abuse
illness	teenage pregnancy
having to earn money	learning disabilities
overworked teachers	boring classes
not caring about school	

The list itself might be useful, but remember that one reason for prewriting is to come up with new ideas, to think about a subject or issue in different ways. This is where cause-and-effect thinking gets interesting.

Whether something is a cause or an effect is sometimes a matter of perspective. It can be said that poverty causes illiteracy. A child might have to go to work to earn money instead of going to school to learn to read. At the same time, this cause-and-effect relationship could be inverted, turned upside down. Then illiteracy would be the cause, and poverty would be the effect. Does illiteracy cause poverty? Yes, a person who cannot read or write would not be hired to do many kinds of work. This person might not be able to find a job.

Illness might cause illiteracy. Someone who is ill much of the time might not attend school regularly. Can illiteracy cause illness? Yes, someone who can't read the directions on the label for using a cleaning product might not know that he or she should use the product only in well-ventilated areas. Then this person's illiteracy could cause serious illness.

2. So, basically, the next step in this prewriting strategy is to look at the causes listed in step 1 and think about how they, the causes, might also be effects. This is harder than it sounds, but it is well worth trying.

There are two pitfalls to watch out for when using this kind of cause-and-effect prewriting. First, almost everything has multiple causes. Therefore, don't just decide that one factor causes a complex problem. Drug abuse may be a cause of illiteracy, and illiteracy may be a cause of drug abuse, but both illiteracy and drug abuse have many other causes.

The second pitfall is being too conventional. Be creative. Look for unusual causes or effects. As mentioned previously, this kind of prewriting can help a writer come up with new ideas. In this kind of prewriting exercise, there are no right or wrong answers. Does poverty cause crime, or does crime cause poverty? The important part of the exercise is the thinking it requires.

WHY PRACTICE PREWRITING?

The eight prewriting strategies presented here for finding new perspectives and ideas, for finding something to say, are only a few out of many useful strategies. Each person thinks differently.

By learning and practicing different thinking and information-gathering strategies, a person becomes capable of more complex thought. Because writers need fresh ideas, perspectives, and opinions, they must be thoughtful and must often be creative.

Many good ideas never become good writing. The best way to test an idea is to write about it without stopping for ten or fifteen minutes. Write quickly and let the ideas take shape. Do not worry about spelling or apostrophes—just write. The trick is to get started. If the nonstop-writing approach isn't going anywhere, or if the writer doesn't like the writing, then nothing is lost. The writer will have more ideas after writing than before and will better understand the subject or issues. That is what prewriting is all about. The more prewriting and the more types of prewriting a writer does, the better.

ACTIVITIES

A. *Working with others*

1. Discuss how the following expressions are oxymoronic. Can you describe situations (using specific details) wherein these would be oxymorons?

defensive weapon	tender ridicule
happy tears	expensive bargain
constant change	learned ignorance
uncontested divorce	safe risk
perfect fool	pretty ugly

2. Discuss what persona would be good to adopt if you were prewriting about each of the following subjects.

teenage alcohol abuse	fuel costs
careers in education	modern art

business etiquette   tax fraud

learning disabilities   TV advertising

clear air

3. Where do other people find their ideas? Are there prewriting strategies one person has that others haven't thought of or don't use? Does everybody think in similar ways, or is thinking different for each thinker? Make a list of ways that people you know remember, find, or invent ideas or perspectives.

4. Read and discuss the following examples of student prewriting. Do they contain ideas for essays? Can the people in the group see potential focuses for essays in these examples of prewriting?

EXAMPLE OF FINDING AN OXYMORON:

Irrational Reasoning

I feel irrational reasoning is an oxymoron because irrational means not to have the power to reason. Lacking reason is unreasonable. Reasoning means to be able to deduce principals from fact and an irrational person would be unable to do this. Using this in a sentence might be like this. The decision Connie made after the accident was due to her irrational reasoning. In this sentence you understand that Connie made an irrational decision but it also says that Connie reasoned out the irrational decision. Connie could not do this since the two words most definitely contradict one another. Yet you can use these two words together and the person reading the sentence seems to get a better understanding of what the writer means.

Barbara B.

122 words

EXAMPLE OF FINDING AN OXYMORON:

Radiation Therapy

One of the most common forms of illness is cancer.
"Radiation Therapy" is what modern medicine prescribes
to combat the presence. In my opinion radiation therapy
needs to be closely examined before undergoing this type
of cancer treatment.

This type of therapy is nothing more than lunacy.
For example a person would not stand inside of a nuclear
reactor during a meltdown. Why? Because of exposure to
nuclear radiation.

Therapy is supposed to treat and induce healing. In
short, to heal whatever ails you.

The example provided over dramatizes the issue for a
reason to think about what is happening to you.

Radiation sickness is a side effect of radiation
treatments commonly characterized by nausea, vomiting,
loss of hair and teeth. It seems strange to me that a
person has to feel sick, puke, lose hair and teeth, all
just to feel better. I think that we're nothing more than
human ginney pigs. Radiation therapy typically destroys
thyroids, liver, and kidneys. Great. Cure the cancer and
the patient dies of kidney failure.

If, as a patient, you blindly follow accepted medical
practices without checking all of the options, why not
wander down to Hanford and save yourself $40,000?

Mark A.
195 words

EXAMPLE OF COINING AN OXYMORON:

Good Pain

When I think of pain, I think of something
uncomfortable, and very unpleasant. The only thing I can

think about is how to relieve the discomfort. This is a
very negative thing to me, and I'm sure for everyone else
as well. But when I think of good, I immediately think of
something pleasant and enjoyable. I usually would like
such a thing to be repeated and enjoyed as much as
possible. A good thing makes me happy, and is very
positive to me. So, how can you have a good pain? I know
some people feel that when they get a massage, and it
hurts a little, they feel that is a good pain, because
they know in the long-run, the pain will be gone, and they
will be relaxed. But, as far as I'm concerned, pain will
always be negative, with no good connotations whatever.

Michelle B.

149 words

EXAMPLE OF COMPARE AND CONTRAST:

Gun and Cigarette

A gun and a cigarette are completely different
things (one is a weapon and the other is just leaves),
their shapes are much different, and also (this is an
interesting difference) a gun is so hard usually, but a
cigarette is soft. There are interesting similarties.
First, both objects are related to fire and smoke. People
need a match or a lighter to start to smoke a cigarette.
Second, both have pretty negative impressions such as
dark, black, death, and so on. It's so easy for us to
imagine that both sometimes lead to death. Third,
children usually don't have these things. These are only
for adults. And, finally, this was my impression when I
saw the movie <u>Platoon</u>. Both are related to soldiers.

Nick V.

126 words

B. *Working alone (prewriting and writing a complete essay)*

1. Read all of your Thursday "Rethinks" so far, and choose one of the issues or opinions you have written about. This issue or opinion is part of the focus for your next essay.

2. Starting with the issue or opinion you have chosen, make a communication situation triangle for your next essay. Remember that an issue, an opinion about it, and an intended audience are the components of a focus.

3. Keeping your communication situation triangle in mind, select and complete three of the following prewriting strategies:

   a. Just plain write what you think about the opinion, issue, or audience you have chosen. Write quickly and don't worry about what you will come up with. Try to be honest.

   b. Write a brief narrative (story) about an incident wherein the character or characters are experiencing some aspect of the focus you have chosen for this essay.

   c. Go to the library and find three articles about the issue you have chosen. Take notes on the articles using the strategies explained in this chapter.

   d. Talk to someone about your project. During the conversation, practice asking for examples, paraphrasing, and asking the other person to expand on his or her comments.

   e. Keeping your issue in mind, create or find three oxymorons, and then write a paragraph on each explaining why or how it is oxymoronic.

   f. In ten minutes, quickly write everything you can think of about what it would be like to be someone with special knowledge or experience about your issue. Then write what that persona would think and say about it.

   g. In ten to fifteen minutes, write everything you can think of comparing two very unlike objects, activities, or situations. Have one of the things you choose be related to your issue and the other completely unrelated. Or, in ten to fifteen minutes, write everything you can think of contrasting two very similar objects, activities, or situations related to your chosen issue.

4. After doing this prewriting, check to see if you have a clear focus for your essay. If not, do more prewriting.

5. Look again at your communication situation triangle and at the other prewriting you have completed; then set it aside and write an essay.

6. Exchange drafts with someone in your class, and make some of the suggestions for improving the drafts presented in the "Rewriting" section of Chapter 2.

7. Using some of these suggestions and other ideas for improvements that you think of, rewrite your essay.

8. Optional: Type up this second draft, proofread it, and submit it to the instructor for additional suggestions on how you might improve it.

5

CONVENTIONAL FORMS

Some Ways to Organize Written Language

"And so you just threw everything together? . . . Mathews, a posse is something you have to organize."

Communication, because it always includes two or more people, requires that the participants follow certain conventions. First of all, they must share a language — must speak or write a language that both understand. You wouldn't, for example, speak French to someone who didn't speak French. When communication is the goal, the people communicating must understand the words being used.

Conversations that go beyond the "How are you?"/"I'm fine." variety also follow certain conventions, although the conventions seem so natural to us that we don't notice them. When talking to friends, it sometimes feels like the conversation is going in several directions all at once, and sometimes it is. Two friends might discuss the weather, then a mutual friend, then some current event they had seen in the news, then another current event, and then return to the weather. These conversations seem unstructured, but they do tend to follow a few conventions. One is that the two people take turns talking and listening. Another is that friends offer each other advice but don't usually order one another around. Yet another convention of conversations between friends is that they don't say unkind things about each other's family members.

When an employer and an employee are talking, there are other conventions. The employer generally does most of the talking, and the employee is expected to listen carefully and make sure he or she understands what the employer is saying or asking. Generally, the employer "controls" the conversation because he or she signs the employee's paychecks. This may or may not be "fair," but it is expected; it is conventional.

Readers have certain expectations when they read. Books are organized into paragraphs, pages, and chapters. Each of these has a beginning, middle, and end, and each part relates to the other parts. You wouldn't, for example, expect to find a chapter about car fanbelts in a book about insulating houses.

Essay writers also follow certain conventions. Every piece of writing is different. At the same time, there are familiar ways to communicate in writing that readers know and almost seem to expect. These conventions (or generally shared reader expectations) concerning the organization of essay writing exist at at least two levels: conventions for individual paragraphs, and conventions concerning the organization of whole essays.

CONVENTIONS CONCERNING THE
ORGANIZATION OF PARAGRAPHS

All essays contain general principles or conclusions and specific facts, details, and examples. Facts, details, and examples are the building blocks of essays. At the paragraph level, general statements serve to organize and make meaning out of the writer's specific facts, details, and examples. By finding and including these components, a writer makes each paragraph of an essay stronger and more believable. For example, writing "Women still do not hold many high management positions in the work force" (*general principle*) is stronger when the writer backs up this general statement with the example, "In the insurance company where I work, over half the employees are women, but all of the managers are men" (*specific example*). The specific example supports the general principle.

It is not enough just to list facts, details, and examples from experience or from articles published in newspapers, magazines, journals, or reports. Writers are expected to organize these resources into paragraphs, and there are two conventional, *logical* operations they can use: inductive and deductive.

Inductive Form: With inductive form, the writer presents facts and examples from experience or from published sources and then writes what they mean to the writer — moving from the specific to the general.

1. Specific facts and examples:
   a. *Specific example:* Last year the required textbook for Math 105 at this school cost nineteen dollars. This year the same book costs twenty-four dollars.
   b. *Specific fact:* College tuition in this state has gone up 30% in the last three years.
   c. *Specific fact:* Interest rates on federally insured student loans have gone up recently.

2. General conclusion drawn from these specific facts and this example: It is getting more expensive to attend college.

A writer using inductive form in a paragraph can also start the paragraph with a general statement and then add facts and examples to support that statement.

1. General statement: Reading a local newspaper is the best way to get good information about current local events.
2. Specific facts and an example:
   a. *Specific fact:* Most TV news is about national and international events.
   b. *Specific fact:* Local TV news includes a little bit of information about many different things.
   c. *Specific example:* In this town, there is no weekly news magazine that reports on local problems and proposed solutions.

The idea is to include facts and examples *and* suggest what they might mean.

Deductive Form: With deductive form, the writer starts with a general statement and then applies it to specific instances — moving from the general to the specific. Usually the general statement is one with which most people would agree.

1. General principle: The most important considerations in maintaining an automobile are those related to safety.
2. Specific applications:
   a. *Specific application:* Good tires are more important for safe driving than a good stereo tapedeck.
   b. *Specific application:* When choosing between getting a crumpled fender straightened and painted or replacing the worn out brakes, fix the brakes.

A paragraph usually includes both the general and the specific. Using inductive or deductive form in a paragraph helps the reader to understand both the writer's opinions and how those opinions are connected to specifics. As a general rule, a fact or example should never stand alone; it either illustrates or shows an application of a general principle (*deductive* form), or it leads the reader toward or supports a general statement (*inductive* form). These two organizing strategies are among the writer's most powerful resources. Readers expect to see them at work in paragraphs. They make it easy for readers to follow the writer's train of thought. Readers also expect paragraphs to be at least forty or fifty words long and to contain four or more sentences.

It is conventional for each paragraph in an essay to include only one general principle or one general statement. Some people call this a *topic sentence*. Not every paragraph will contain a topic sentence, but many will. Words can be defined, and sentences conventionally express a complete thought; as a general rule, however, the smallest block of meaning in an essay is the paragraph.

By this time, you have practiced writing many types of units, or clusters of several paragraphs each. Each cluster is not an essay, but each could be useful to a writer who is trying to find a focus for an essay, and some clusters could even become parts of a complete essay.

1. In your journal (Chapter 1), you have done various types of writing several times:
   1.1 Mondays: "What I really think about. . . ." In these short pieces, you have expressed *your* opinions about issues important to you. By doing so, you have clarified your own thinking. This is part of finding a focus.
   1.2 Tuesdays: "The letter I should probably write." In these efforts, you have practiced sharing your experiences and opinions with a real audience. Identifying an intended audience is also part of finding a focus for an essay.
   1.3 Wednesdays: On Wednesdays you have read an article, briefly summarized its contents, and then responded to those contents in terms of what they mean to you. The written results of these efforts might serve as units or clusters of paragraphs that you could include in an essay.

    1.4 Thursdays: "Rethink." Once a week, you have chosen one of your ideas and expanded on it by adding details and examples to help a reader understand both your idea and the reasons behind it. In a way, "Rethinks" are a kind of "mini-essay."

2. You have also practiced several other kinds of thinking and writing, each of which is a way to gather and generate the raw materials out of which essays are made. As suggested in Chapter 4, you have done some of the following:

    2.1 You have used the same skills that you developed by writing Monday journal entries to find and examine what you think about specific subjects and issues.

    2.2 You have written short narratives (stories) about incidents related to a subject or issue.

    2.3 You have practiced taking notes on articles you have read, notes that clearly show which of the facts, opinions, and details are

        a. quotations, "the author's content in the author's own words";

        b. paraphrases, the author's material but in your own words; and

        c. your responses to the author's material, [what you think while reading and thinking about what you are reading].

    2.4 You have talked with people about issues on which they are experts, and you have taken clear notes on those conversations.

    2.5 You have used oxymorons in two ways:

        a. You have looked for oxymorons that people already use, such as "diet candy" and "inexpensive car."

        b. You have made up oxymorons by putting two words together that are normally considered contradictory, such as "honest deception" and "safe risk."

    2.6 You have looked at issues from someone else's perspective by adopting a persona in two ways:

        a. writing the opposite of what you really think, and

        b. imagining that you are someone more centrally concerned with an issue than you are, and writing about it from that person's perspective.

2.7 You have done comparative analysis (compare and contrast) in two ways:
   a. looking at and writing about the *differences* between two things that are *similar*, and
   b. looking at and writing about the *similarities* between two things that are very *different*.

2.8 You have used causal analysis (cause and effect) to consider the sources of a problem and any other kinds of problems that are related to it.

The point is that *you have been writing these units.* You have been practicing looking at issues from different perspectives, gathering facts, details, and examples, and organizing these into paragraphs and units comprised of several paragraphs each.

Each of these types of journal writing and kinds of prewriting can be seen as ways of finding, supporting, or developing a focus for an essay; each could be thought of as a tool in a box of tools. Like carpenters or auto mechanics who choose the tools that fit the jobs they are working on, writers choose resources that fit communication situations.

There are no dependable formulas for putting together an essay, but there are good working principles. One is to select and use in each essay three or four of the resources in the foregoing list. The idea is to choose the resources that best meet the needs of the writer's focus, those that fit the writing situation (communication situation). Then the writer writes these units or clusters of related paragraphs. They later become the middle of his or her essay.

CONVENTIONS CONCERNING THE ORGANIZATION OF ESSAYS

Just as there are conventional or expected ways to organize paragraphs, there are conventional ways to organize essays. Newspaper writers (journalists) often use a conventional form called the *inverted triangle.*

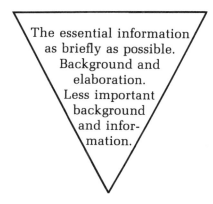

The essential information as briefly as possible. Background and elaboration. Less important background and information.

This form helps the reader. The first paragraphs in a news article give a *nutshell* of the news story as a whole (who, what, when, where, and how), so a newspaper reader can read just those early paragraphs and get the important information. If readers want to know more, they can read the whole article.

Another conventional form is the five-paragraph essay. This used to be popular in high-school and college writing courses and is still a fair way to go in some writing situations — especially when time pressures are intense. For example, a student asked to write three short essays in a one-hour, essay-exam situation could write three five-paragraph essays. Five-paragraph essays are organized as follows:

Paragraph 1: (Introduction) Tell the reader what you are writing about and three points you will make in the essay.
Paragraph 2: Discuss the first of your three points.
Paragraph 3: Discuss the second of your three points.
Paragraph 4: Discuss your third point.
Paragraph 5: (Conclusion) Tell the reader what you have just discussed (points one, two, and three).

Most people think this conventional form is limited. One problem is that it is repetitious. Does a writer need to announce what he or she will say, say it, then tell the reader again what has just been said? Another problem with the five-paragraph essay is that it is often difficult to find an issue small enough to cover in five paragraphs. Everyone should know how to write a five-paragraph essay, but every writer should be aware that it is only one of many conventional forms and that other forms are often more interesting and more readable.

The five-paragraph essay does, however, help writers to understand some basic principles for organizing an essay. It helps them to realize that most essays have introductions, middles, and conclusions.

1. **Introductions:** Essay introductions are usually one or two paragraphs. They usually alert the reader to the writer's focus (issue, writer's opinion(s) about the issue, and intended audience). Many times an introduction is narrative — it describes an incident or situation so that the reader knows from the very start what the essay will be about. In another conventional type of introduction, the writer introduces the issue by defining it with specific facts or statistics. The writer wants to capture the reader's attention and hopes the reader will *want* to read the whole essay.

2. **Middles:** The middle, or body, of an essay is the largest section. Most pieces of writing are longer than one paragraph. Essays are usually made up of several clusters of two or more paragraphs each. Each cluster addresses the essay's focus (issue, author's opinion(s) about the issue, and the author's intended audience) from a different angle or perspective. Just as a paragraph applies a general principle to specific details and examples (deductive form) or includes specific details and examples that lead to a general conclusion (inductive form), an essay contains several clusters of paragraphs, all of which support or develop the essay's focus. These larger units of meaning, these cluster's of two or more paragraphs, are the components of the middle part of an essay.

3. **Conclusions:** After an author has the middle of an essay written, it is time to write a conclusion. Usually an essay's conclusion contains a brief summary of the essay's focus and of the author's major units or clusters of related paragraphs. It is also conventional to include some advice to the reader for further thought or action.

PLANNING THE ESSAY:
Matching Prewriting to
the Communication Situation

Example 1: Harmful Chemicals

Suppose that a student is asked to write something about harmful chemicals in the environment. He first considers the elements of the communication situation discussed earlier: (1) issue; (2) desired effect or purpose of the essay; (3) audience; (4) how the writer wants to present him or herself; and (5) (optional) timing.

The student wants to write something different, so he decides not to write about nuclear waste, the ozone layer, or acid rain. He thinks about what chemicals have harmed him, and he gets an idea. He was once a sugar addict; he used to buy packages of Auntie Jan's Peanut Cluster Cookies and eat all the cookies himself. He used to buy one-pound packages of chocolate-coated peanuts and eat them in an hour. He began to experience health difficulties. A healthcare professional told him that his sugar habit was the principal cause of his health problems and that, in addition to problems with weight control, skin complexion, and tooth decay, excessive sugar consumption contributed to such larger problems as diabetes and heart disease.

While prewriting, the writer remembers this information and comes up with the oxymoron "deadly cookies." He also remembers the medical professional saying that eating too much sugar was as bad for him as smoking cigarettes. So the writer decides that tobacco and sugar *are* harmful chemicals in the environment. His *purpose* then becomes convincing the audience of the truth of this perspective.

Next, he needs to identify an intended audience. He thinks of people he knows who are aware of the harmful effects of tobacco but who consume large quantities of cookies, cake, ice cream, and soda pop. These people do not read the ingredients listed on the packages of the foods they buy at the grocery store, so they are not aware of how much additional sugar there is in many processed foods.

The writer then thinks about how to present himself in this essay. He has never used tobacco products, but he considers himself a reformed sugar addict. He decides to *present himself* as someone concerned with other people's health as well as his own. As for timing, he knows that it is always good to complete assignments before they are due. Having gotten this far, the writer plans his prewriting by choosing from among the types of prewriting he has been doing.

The writer knows that he needs to write an introduction that alerts the reader to the issue in question and wins the reader's attention. He decides to tell a story (narrative), so he tells about his last visit to a movie theater. He describes the little piles of cigarette butts scattered around the theater entrance, and the munching and crunching of popcorn and chocolate-coated peanuts and the slurping of soft drinks he heard while trying to watch and hear the movie. He does this in two or three paragraphs — unit one. The intended audience that he imagines hates tobacco smoke but thinks chocolate is one of the four major food groups.

He next writes a section of four or five paragraphs that compare and contrast tobacco use and the eating of products that contain sugar. He talks about how people can become addicted to cigarettes or to sugar and about polluting the human body with both — unit two.

Next the writer wants to do some reading, so he finds an article or two each about the effects of cigarette smoking and the effects of eating sugar. He organizes this data and writes another cluster of related paragraphs — unit three.

By this time, he feels that he has written quite a bit and wants to wrap it all up. Because he has done this much work already, he has earned the right to offer some advice. So the last cluster of paragraphs in the essay is his advice to the reader on the uses and abuses of tobacco and sugar.

Keep in mind that this person has written only a very rough initial draft. He still needs to rewrite the draft (at least twice) to refine and polish his essay (discussed later in this book). But by making and using a plan — by examining the communication situation and then carefully choosing the units — he has made the essay easier for him to write and for others to read.

An outline of his essay would look like this:

```
Narration (Introduction)
(the writer's visit
to a movie theater)
```

```
Compare and Contrast
(sugar and tobacco)
```

```
Summary
(facts and details found in
published articles)
```

```
Conclusion
(advice about consuming
tobacco and sugar)
```

Remember that the units, the resources, a writer chooses always depend on the communication situation.

Example 2: Higher Education

Suppose that a student has been asked to write something about education. She knows that education is a very large subject; there are literally thousands of new books and articles published about education each year, each of which deals with a very small and well-defined aspect of education. She knows that she can't write about education in general, so she thinks about college education and, more specifically, about the costs of higher education. She has completed one year of her own college education and considers herself an expert in writing checks for tuition, books, rent, school supplies, food, and special course and lab fees. Her audience is other people who, like herself, will try to pay their way through college by working nights at fast-food restaurants and self-service gas stations. She wants her audience to know what to expect. This, then, is the communication situation.

The writer isn't sure how much her year of college has cost, so she looks through her check registers for the past year. She separates her expenses into categories and subcategories. Her categories are "School-related Payments" and "Living Expenses." Under the school-related category, she has four subcategories: tuition, books, other fees, and supplies. The subcategories under living expenses are rent, food, phone, energy costs, and transportation. This prewriting completed, she is ready to choose and write the units of her essay.

1. The first unit or introduction will be a *definition* of her present financial resources — income, savings, and loans.
2. The second unit will include details and facts about what it costs her (or any other college student) to live (inexpensively).
3. The third part will cover what it costs her, beyond her living expenses, to go to college (more facts and details).
4. The fourth unit will be her conclusion, in which she will recommend ways to plan for the costs discussed earlier.

She is tempted to add a fifth cluster of paragraphs in which she would discuss causes and effects. What happens when a check written to the telephone company bounces, for instance, or what exactly is bankruptcy? She decides not to do this, however, because she wants her audience to take her seriously.

At any rate, she has a plan for her essay and is ready to write an initial draft. She may or may not follow her plan exactly, but having the plan is a distinct advantage.

An outline of her essay would look like this:

```
Definition (Introduction)
(the writer's
economic situation)
```

Details and Facts
(living expenses)

Details and Facts
(beyond her living expenses,
what it costs her to go
to college)

Conclusion
(the writer's summary of what costs
her audience should expect
when they go to college and her
advice about meeting these expenses)

SUGGESTIONS FOR PLANNING ESSAYS

1. Do not expect to draw only upon memory as a resource for writing. Libraries are full of useful and accessible facts, opinions, and statistics; find them and use them. Also, communities in general and universities and community colleges in particular are full of experts; talk to them.
2. Vary the units you use in any given essay. For example, do not make all four or five units of your essay cause and effect.
3. Vary the essays you write. It is tempting to design a formula of units and then use it every time you write an essay. Variety is the spice of writing as well as of life.
4. Try to make units of approximately equal length. This adds symmetry, or balance, to your presentation. Conclusions and introductions are usually smaller than the units that make up the middle, or body, of your essay.

5. Many writers wait until they have written a whole initial draft before writing an introduction to that draft. This can be a good strategy. The introduction to an essay alerts the reader to the essay's focus. Sometimes the focus for an essay changes while the writer is writing the essay.

6. Just because you have a plan doesn't mean that you have to follow it. If the initial draft you write doesn't reflect your plan, judge it on its own merits rather than on whether it matches your plan.

7. Keep your prewriting time short. It is easy to put off the actual writing by spending hours, days, weeks, or months planning to write.

8. Remember that each unit or cluster of paragraphs you write should relate to the focus of your essay; as a general rule, you should mention this focus again in each unit.

Planning and writing units comprised of related paragraphs, each of which supports or develops the focus of your essay, is not the only way to approach an essay-writing project, but it is one way writers get a first full draft of an essay down on paper or into a word processor. For most people, writing that first draft is the hardest part. Once written, a draft can always be improved.

NOTE TO THE READER

Many times, when a writer has done a thorough job of planning and prewriting an essay, the resulting initial draft is well organized. Not all essays are either five-paragraph essays or collections of identifiable units. There are other ordering principles that hold essays together.

At the same time, knowing how to choose, produce, and arrange clusters of related paragraphs for an essay is a valuable strategy for a writer. Writers should understand and use this strategy, even though they might not use it every time they write an essay. Selecting, producing, and arranging units comprised of several paragraphs each is an especially effective approach for writers asked to write long essays. For many writers, a fifteen- or twenty-page essay or research project is terrifying. By breaking such a project down into smaller parts, however, the writer can reduce his or her anxiety and get to work on the project.

ACTIVITIES

A. *Working with others*
   1. Discuss what other things (types of units or clusters of related paragraphs) one can do with written language in addition to those listed in this chapter, and then make a list of these additional resources.
   2. Find an essay that you enjoy, make copies for the people you write with, and then together identify the units it contains.

B. *Working alone*
   1. Organize facts:
      a. Categorize, classify, and subordinate your living expenses for last month or last year.
      b. If you watch TV, buy a program guide and mark each program you watch in one week. Then categorize, classify, and subordinate the programs you watched.
   2. Plan and write an essay:
      a. After you have defined a particular communication situation, choose four or five resources, or units, that you might employ in an essay. Practice may not make perfect, but the more plans you have made, the easier (and quicker) you will be able to make such plans.
      b. Write an initial draft of the essay you planned in Activity **B.2.a.**
   3. Write a five-paragraph essay.
   4. Analyze and rewrite one of your essays. Outline the units

it contains. What do you "do" in each section or paragraph? Then look at your outline to see if *you* think a unit should be added or deleted. Is there a part that tries to do too much and should be divided into two? Is each section about the same size (number of words) as the others? Based on your analysis of the units, rewrite your essay to make it better.

Chapter 6

PLANNING AND PREWRITING THE LONGER ESSAY

Two Case Studies

"Say . . . Now THERE'S a little hat!"

One of the biggest dangers for a person reading about writing is interpreting suggestions about what he or she *can* or *may do* as orders telling what *must be done*. It would be easier if there were just *one* right way to write, but there is not. Each time a person is asked to write or just plain decides to write something, the situation is different. If writing the same paper over and over was what writing was all about, then what would be the point? Writing is a means for expressing new thoughts, opinions, and perspectives, for communicating what the writer thinks.

Originally, the word *essay* meant "to try." "To try" can mean "to attempt," but it can also mean "to try out." Earlier in this book, I reminded the reader that essays contain opinions, that an essay is the writer's opinion or opinions and the reasons behind them. To go one step further, then, *an essay can be seen as a person's efforts "to try out" an idea or an opinion.*

We all have opinions. We all have ideas. We get them from experience, from other people, from what we read, and from our own thinking. Looking closely at our opinions and ideas to understand why we have them is central to the process of writing essays. This book is about finding, examining, and communicating those opinions and ideas.

By this time, those readers who have been doing the recommended Activities at the ends of chapters — those who have been writing and talking about ideas and opinions and about writing — should be ready to prepare for writing a longer essay, a paper containing more than one thousand words.

Some people think there are two distinct reasons for writing papers: (1) people write because they have to (to satisfy some sort of supervisor or instructor); and (2) people write because they feel they need to, because they have something important to communicate. These do not have to be seen as different categories; even when people are required to write, they can think of the project as an opportunity to communicate ideas and opinions that are important to them. Good writers put themselves into every essay they write. It is not enough to satisfy a teacher or a supervisor; writers need to satisfy themselves.

In order to do their best, to satisfy themselves, writers need to *prepare* to write by gathering information, examining opinions, and playing with ideas. This is what writers do. What follows are two examples of writers preparing themselves to write longer essays. Once again, the strategies used by these writers are not things a person *must do*; they are strategies a writer *may do*. The point is that the writer takes the time and energy that *he or she needs* to get ready to write.

Preparing to write an essay can be very much like doing the daily writing tasks discussed in Chapter 1 of this book. Just as it is better to write for fifteen or twenty minutes each day than to spend three hours doing a week's worth of daily writing all at once, it is better to work on an essay project for about an hour a day for five days than to spend five hours on the project the night before it is due. Writing essays requires thinking, and thinking takes time.

CASE STUDY 1:
Writing for a College Course

For the purposes here, let's imagine that a student whose name is Jerry has been asked to write a paper for a college course. Furthermore, let's imagine that it is a sophomore-level political science course and that the instructor has specified that the students write about the subject "U.S. Militay Aid to Third World Countries." The instructor has also required that the essay be three to six typed, double-spaced, pages long.

Jerry knows he will not do very well if he procrastinates. He has two weeks to complete the project, and he starts working on it the day it is first mentioned by the instructor.

Day 1: Jerry knows he can't cover everything there is to know or say about "U.S. Military Aid to the Third World," so he tries some of the prewriting strategies discussed earlier in this book. First Jerry brainstorms for relevant oxymorons; he plays with ideas. "Defensive weapon" seems like an oxymoron to him, so he writes it down. He also comes up with "limited nuclear war," "surgical bombing," "honest dictator," "partial victory," and "machine guns for peace."

Satisfied with these oxymorons, Jerry is ready to start on his own sequence of short writing efforts — his units — which may or may not later fit into his essay. The toughest aspect of writing, for most people, is getting started, so Jerry will just plain start. He keeps his tasks small and his expectations low.

The first unit is a written exploration of one of his oxymorons. Jerry likes the contradiction implied in the phrase "machine guns for peace," so he writes about it, without stopping, for ten or fifteen minutes. As when he does his daily writing assignments (see Chapter 1), he writes quickly and *does not* worry about spelling, punctuation, and grammar. He simply writes. When the time is up, he puts his oxymorons and the writing he has done in a folder and lays it aside.

Day 2: Next Jerry decides to adopt a persona. He's still thinking about machine guns — Uzis, M-16s, AK-47s, M-3s — and he has discovered that one sad fact about weapons is that when they are around, people use them.

As explained earlier, adopting a persona requires that the writer imagine he is someone he is not. Jerry decides to imagine that he is a Nicaraguan (or Lebanese, or Honduran, or Nigerian) peasant woman. He is going to write the opposite of what he really thinks, so, using what he imagines to be the voice of the Nicaraguan peasant woman, he writes about the benefits of having many machine guns around her village. He writes about how handy a machine gun is when one is trying to grow corn. He discusses the joys of having one's crops and home burned down by men and women who walk around the countryside heavily armed. It is certainly convenient, he writes, when all the men and many of the women of the village are either dead or off somewhere carrying weapons around looking for reasons to shoot them. Jerry doesn't believe these things; he is playing with ideas. Jerry then puts this work in his folder and lays it aside.

Day 3: Jerry goes to the library and finds three recent articles about weapons and Third World countries. There are many such articles; there are many guns in the so-called developing nations. He reads the articles and takes notes on them. Then he responds in writing, for ten to fifteen minutes, to each of the articles. He adds these materials to his folder.

Day 4:   Because one of the articles Jerry read on Day 3 focused on the economic hardships of war, he brainstorms a list of causes and effects of economic hardships in small communities that depend on farming for their economic well-being. He then inverts the cause-and-effect relationships on his list, looking to see if some of the causes can be seen as effects and if some of the effects can be seen as causes.

As mentioned earlier in this book, a writer should remember that what one person sees as a cause might be seen as an effect by another person. Cause-and-effect thinking is mostly a matter of perspective. Someone could say that money problems cause divorce. Another person could say that divorce causes money problems. Both would be right. It depends on how you look at the issue. It is sometimes helpful to call an obvious cause an effect, and then think about what causes it, or to call an effect a cause, and then consider what effects it has. For example, war causes hardships, but hardships might cause war.

After he has thought about causes and effects and made some notes about them, Jerry writes for ten to fifteen minutes about some of the causes and effects of economic hardships in Third World countries. These materials also go into his folder.

Day 5:   Jerry needs to create a focus for his essay. He looks over all the materials in his folder and considers the five factors of his communication situation: (1) What is his issue? (2) What does he hope to achieve by writing this essay (purpose)? (3) Who is his intended audience, and what are that audience's feelings and opinions about his subject? (4) How does he want his audience to perceive him; how does he want to present himself? and (5) (optional) Can he use the notion of timing to make his writing efforts more successful?

At this stage of prewriting, it would probably be wise for Jerry to consider several different communication situations, to make two or three different communication situation triangles. He might also look over all the prewriting he has done and think about what kinds of units would best be included in his essay and in what order; this step is not always helpful, but for a long essay it is a good idea because it helps the writer to control the material.

For most people, the more time they spend preparing to write an essay, the easier it is for them to write it; being prepared saves time in the long run. Not preparing enough before starting to write is one of the biggest problems faced by inexperienced writers. Fortunately for Jerry, he has worked for about an hour each day for five days, and he is now ready to write a draft. He chose to do several kinds of prewriting to help him get ready to write; he could have chosen others. The idea is to choose the kinds of short writing tasks that fit the issue, the writer's opinion, and the needs of the audience to whom the writer is writing. The idea is to be prepared. Jerry has done this. He still has to write the initial draft of his essay, but since he has started early, he has plenty of time. Jerry may have done more preparation than he will use in his essay, but he has not wasted any time. Because he has thought and written about his issue several times, he understands it better. By this time, he probably has some very good ideas for the essay he wants to write.

CASE STUDY 2:
Writing for a College Course
and Writing for Yourself

Julie is a student in a freshman composition course. Her teacher announces the subject area for the next paper—Drug Abuse. Julie is an expert on drug abuse, although she may never have thought about it in this way. She has an alcoholic parent. Alcohol abuse, people are starting to recognize, is the biggest drug problem in this country and probably in the world.

This case study shows how risky writing can be. It takes real courage, but Julie decides to write not only for the teacher but also for herself.

Day 1: Julie decides to start by adopting a persona. She imagines what an alcoholic would say about his or her habit. Alcoholism is a strange disease. Part of the disease is denying it. People who have a problem with alcohol lose perspective and mistake effects for causes. Some alcoholics believe that they drink because they don't have any friends; it is more likely that these people don't have many friends because they drink too much. Anyway, Julie decides to write for ten or fifteen minutes using what she imagines to be the voice of an alcoholic.

Example of Adopting a Persona
(Pretending to be someone other than yourself)

I have been drinking since I was in high school. Coming from a small town where all we did on weekends was go drinking, I grew up in an environment where everyone drank. And now you expect me to admit that I have a drinking problem after I have been drinking for so many years?

Your mother has driven me to drink a great deal. She always expects so much out of me that I can't handle it. I then get mad and go out and drink, but only a couple of drinks. Not as many as your mother says I have.

At work I have a lot of pressures. My boss is loading more work on me because I get the job done. They are trying to tell me how I can use my vacation time. All of this is building up inside and I need a drink to relax and unwind from the day.

You kids are siding with your mother, so you give me no other choice but to lie and hide the alcohol since you tell her. The way you kids act drives me to drink.

What would the holidays be without drinking? That's why they say at Christmas time to ''drink and be merry.'' One little drink isn't going to hurt anyone. And you had better not tell your mom or else.

I don't drink that much, and I know when I have had
enough. And I am very capable of driving.
    I wish people would just let me alone to do my own
thing.

Julie puts this writing in a folder and sets it side.

Day 2:   Because she has strong attitudes and opinions about
alcoholism, Julie next chooses to write for ten or fifteen minutes
using the opposite viewpoint of what she really believes; this is
another way to adopt a persona. As mentioned before, when a
writer has strong opinions about a subject, it is often useful for
that person to write from the opposite viewpoint. By doing this,
the writer has a chance to see more clearly the other side of an
issue.

Example of Adopting a Persona
(The opposite of what the writer believes)

    Alcoholism isn't a problem in our society. Not that
many people drink. And the people that do drink have
wonderful lives. They don't act any different, and they
don't feel any different about people. Alcohol makes
them better persons. They don't have a problem in the
world.
    When they have been drinking it's perfectly alright
for them to get in their cars and drive, and if they
happen to kill a person because they didn't see that
person walking in the crosswalk where there was a bright
red light hanging above which means ''stop,'' it's no big
deal. It is just one less person they have to worry about
being in their way for the next time that they get in
their car after drinking.
    Your family loves it when you come home drunk and
have the distinct smell of beer on your breath, and your
clothes have the smell of four different kinds of
cigarette smoke. And it just wouldn't be the same if you

didn't yell at your wife and kids. They would think you
were mad at them if you didn't yell at them and call them
names.

An alcoholic should be able to go and spend money
that he doesn't have on alcohol. The family should
realize that booze is much more important than food,
clothing, or shelter.

It's alright for an alcoholic to lie to his boss and
tell him he won't be there today because he has the flu,
when really all it is is a hangover.

An alcoholic should be able to do what he wants while
a person who doesn't drink should go and get some kind of
treatment.

Julie then puts this piece of writing in her folder and lays it aside.

Day 3:   Every writing project is different. Because she has
lived with an alcoholic, Julie has, without intending to, been
preparing to write an essay about alcoholism for a long time. She
has thought and worried about alcoholism. She has read about it
and talked to other people about it. She is an expert on how
alcoholism affects a family. So examining the communication
situation for her essay is easy. She creates a communication
situation triangle (see Figure 6.1, p. 104) and adds it to her folder.

Day 4:   Having come this far, Julie is ready to write a first
draft of her essay. She is well prepared to do so. She has the
advantage of writing about something she knows and cares about;
she has something real to communicate.

Julie begins by finding a quiet working place, turns on her
word processor, looks over all the materials in her folder, and
starts writing. She writes fast, and she writes what she really
thinks. She does not worry about spelling and punctuation. At
this stage of writing an essay, she concentrates on what she is
saying rather than on the rules of grammar; she concentrates on
communicating.

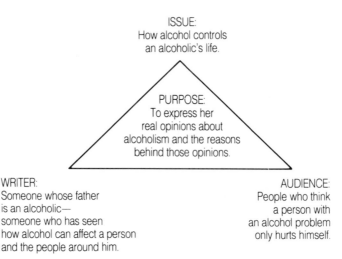

ISSUE:
How alcohol controls
an alcoholic's life.

PURPOSE:
To express her
real opinions about
alcoholism and the reasons
behind those opinions.

WRITER:
Someone whose father
is an alcoholic—
someone who has seen
how alcohol can affect a person
and the people around him.

AUDIENCE:
People who think
a person with
an alcohol problem
only hurts himself.

Figure 6.1

Julie knows she will make changes in her draft later, so she leaves a side margin by writing only on the right-hand two-thirds of each sheet of paper. The following is her first draft.

> Alcoholism is a disease that takes control of your life in many ways.
>
> Alcohol doesn't only ruin the life of the person consuming the alcohol, but the people who come in close contact are also affected. This plays a big role in that little children see their parents living on a bottle day after day. When they

grow up they start to wonder whether
they too will become an alcoholics.
The children are even embarrassed
about their parents for the way they
act when they come in close contact
with their friends.

When they drink they're a
totally different person. The
alcohol has a effect on them that
causes them not only to be mean, not
only physically but mentally as
well. A lot of times they yell at
their families by telling them they
are worthless and he deserves
better. The name calling gets
worse. This leaves scars forever!
They will never forget how the
alcoholic ruined their holidays by
calling them names and making a fool
out of himself. They remember how
when friends were over they would
come in drunk and embarrass you by
yelling at you and tripping over
furniture.

They have a different out look
about life. They tell you that they

don't care about dying. It's going
to happen so when it does, so what?
They have a different outlook on
people. They are very defensive
about what people say. They're very
bitter towards everyone and only
think of themselves. They forget
that people who love him, and will
try and help him get better. But
people who are alcoholics forget
that at one time they too loved the
people who are trying to help him,
and all they do is pull away from the
ones they loved and get closer to
alcohol.

They are very selfish. Their
money will never be used to buy food,
clothing, or pay bills before they
go and buy a six pack of Coors. He
doesn't care if he doesn't eat. He
figures he gets all his nuritiments
from the alcohol. His clothes become
dirty and old with holes sneaking
about. The money he is using isn't

only his, but his family's, and if
they go without it's alright just as
long as he gets his alcohol.

Working isn't that important to
him. They call in sick quite a bit
and really all it is is a bad hangover
or their just too lazy to get out of
bed. Soon this becomes a habit and he
gets fired for never going to work
anymore. Most alcoholics end up
with no money because they have
spent their last pennie on alcohol.
This not only being lazy doesn't
only cause him to lose his job but
his family as well.

They will lie to their familys
and themselves. They tell their
families that they don't have a
drinking problem. When they know
deep down inside they do. They lie
about how much they have to drink.
They tell them they have only had a
couple of drinks. When really his
family knows he has had more by the

way he is acting and tumbling over
his own two feet. He tells his
family he is going to quit so he
hides so they think he has not been
drinking. But, it catches up with
him when he gets caught.

Alcoholism is a problem that
just doesn't go away. Unless a
person realizes that he or she is an
alcoholic, and reaches out for
help. They will be living in a world
of their own with no family, no job,
and no self-esteem!

Julie is not finished with her essay yet, but because she
prepared herself to write before writing she has a good initial, or
first, draft. She can make it even better. The following chapter is
about how to make a good draft better.

ACTIVITIES

A. *Working with others*

1. Share your list of ways of preparing to write with the
people you write with. Do they have strategies that you
might use? Can you give them some ideas they haven't
thought of?

2. Once each group member has chosen an issue to write

about, discuss which ways of preparing to write (prewriting) might be best for each issue.

3. Prepare a communication situation triangle for your essay; then share it with your writing group. Will your plan work? Can others make useful suggestions about it?

B. *Working alone: Planning and writing another essay*

1. Make your own list of all the ways you can think of to prepare yourself to write an essay.

2. Choose an issue to write an essay about; then choose four of the strategies from the list you have just made that will help you to prepare to write your essay. Your notebook full of daily writing is a good place to look for this issue.

3. Follow through on the four prewriting strategies you have selected to prepare yourself to write your essay.

4. After you have completed the four prewriting strategies, make a communication situation triangle specifying issue, purpose, audience, and how you intend to present yourself in the essay.

5. Write a draft of the essay.

7

COLLABORATION
Writing a Draft and Getting Help on Your Draft from Others

"Wait! Wait! . . . Cancel that, I
guess it says 'helf.'"

Some people can think through their subjects, organize essays in
their heads, and then simply write the final products. Most people most of the time, however, need to do several drafts of an
essay before they are satisfied with it. As a general rule, *anything
worth writing is worth writing three times.* For personal letters and

some business writing, one draft can be enough, but professional writers nearly always write multiple drafts. Many people say that they don't know what they are going to write until they have written it. When Donald Murray, an authority on teaching writing, says that "writing is rewriting," at least part of what he means is that a good essay often becomes something different than what the author had planned on, and therefore needs to be rethought and rewritten after the initial or first draft. In addition, Murray knows that it is easier to work with words already on paper or in a personal computer than with ideas that are still only in the writer's head. This chapter covers a procedure for getting ideas into shape. Note that the procedure is only one possibility among many, and there is not always enough time and energy to do all of the steps.

Assume that a writer has thought about a subject and completed several activities to help generate and organize thoughts. He or she has made outlines, brainstormed, coined oxymorons, compared and contrasted something related to the subject with something completely unrelated, adopted a persona, talked with others, written some units (or clusters of related paragraphs), and employed other prewriting strategies. The writer then examines the communication situation for the essay by considering the issue he or she has chosen to write about, the desired effect(s) of the essay (purpose), the audience, how the writer wants to be perceived by the audience, and timing—in addition to all these other thoughts about the project.

After the writer has done these things, he or she is ready to write. This person looks over this prewriting and then sets it aside. This writer is ready for initial drafting.

INITIAL DRAFTING

People use many ways to get that first draft down on paper or into a personal computer. The goal is to produce a draft. The following are pointers on how to produce it:

1. Roland K. Huff, an expert on teaching writing, suggests that the writer start, as Julie did in the previous chapter, by widening the left-hand margin of lined paper to about one-third of the page width, making that margin three to four inches wide instead of the customary inch or inch and a half. The idea is to leave enough space so that the writer can add examples or move paragraphs around later without having to copy over the portions of the draft that he or she already likes. Most word-processing software also makes this kind of formatting possible.

2. The writer then writes the initial draft. He or she sits down in a comfortable and quiet place where there won't be interruptions. The writer sets aside about an hour, then writes, hard and fast, for that hour. He or she tries to get as many ideas down on paper as possible and *does not* think or worry about spelling, punctuation, or grammar. He or she wants to get a beginning, middle, and end to the draft—*all at once*. A writer should probably not look back at notes or an outline at this time but, rather, just say what needs to be said—on paper.

3. Next the writer should set the initial draft aside for a while—at least twenty-four hours (when possible). He or she lets the draft "cool off." Most writers can't improve a piece of writing right after they have written it. Later on they can be more objective. Because it is easier to read and respond to typed drafts, many writers will type their initial drafts during this "incubation" time.

COLLABORATION: Help That Helps

Perhaps the hardest part of writing is looking at a draft of an essay and making suggestions about how to make it better. Fortunately, most people can see the areas that would benefit from rewriting in someone else's drafts that they cannot see in their own. Somehow writers seem to think that if they know what they mean, then what they have written will communicate that meaning to others. Often this is not the case. On the positive side, writers who practice advising other writers on how to improve their drafts learn, in the process of reading and advising, how to see more clearly the need to rewrite their own drafts.

Those who have been working by themselves and with others on the Activities in this book already have some of the skills and attitudes an editor needs. They are ready to be editors, ready to help one another make their drafts better. The danger is that they will remember the types of things other people in the past have written on their essays (like "*awkward,*" "*fragment,*" and "*comma splice*") and want to write those things. Being an editor does not mean marking someone else's spelling errors or telling someone his or her sentences are "awkward." A good editor makes comments on what in the draft can be improved. The editor's job is to help the writer better communicate what the writer wants to communicate. The following are guidelines for doing just that.

The Role of the Editor

Let us look for a moment at what an editor does. He or she should be an objective responder to a draft. The editor, to be effective, must keep a few things in mind in order to remain objective:

1. The editor's job is to suggest ways that the author can better say what he or she has written. It is not the editor's job to change the writer's mind or to get the writer to agree with the editor.
2. The editor should limit his or her suggestions for improving the draft to two or three. Too much advice tends to confuse rather than help the writer.
3. The editor's comments should point to specific parts of the draft. Comments like "your discussion is too general" are not as helpful as comments like "on page two, in paragraphs four and five, you need to add an example or two because, as reader, I'm not sure what you are saying."

4. A good editor can help a writer improve a draft even when the editor disagrees with what the writer is saying. The editor's task is not to judge right from wrong. People see things from different angles, or perspectives. People have their own opinions. When two people do not agree, it is not because one is right and the other is wrong; rather, the opinions of the two people are simply different.

The Role of the Writer in an Editorial Relationship

The writer must also follow a few simple rules:

1. The editor should not be perceived as an absolute authority. The editor only makes *suggestions*. It is the writer's job to decide which of the editor's suggestions are useful. The editor says what the author *might* do, not what he or she *must* do.
2. When reading or hearing advice from an editor, the writer should overcome the temptation to make excuses. Peter Elbow, another expert on teaching writing, made this observation years ago. It is natural to respond to an editor with comments like, "What I *meant* to say was . . ." or "I wrote this Sunday at midnight, so what do you expect?" These kinds of responses are not helpful. The writer should listen to the editor and perhaps note down some of the editor's comments, but he or she should not be defensive or argumentative.
3. The writer should not change a draft right after hearing comments from an editor. The author should think about the editorial advice before making any of the suggested changes.
4. As a general rule, twenty to fifty percent of an editor's advice will be useful to a writer. Do not expect to let an editor make the decisions. The writer's draft is the writer's property, and *the writer* makes all the decisions about improving the draft.

EDITORIAL RESPONSE TO
INITIAL DRAFTING

Once a writer has an initial, or first, draft, it is time to use an editor. Of course, if the writer rereads a draft and feels that it does not say what he or she wants it to, or if the writer feels that the draft can be improved without an editor's help, that writer might well do some additional work before requesting suggestions from someone else. One of the toughest things a writer has to do is to decide whether a draft is working. If the writer decides that a draft isn't very good or isn't "going anywhere," then the writer should review all the prewriting he or she has done on the project so far and write a brand new initial draft. On the other hand, when the writer decides that an initial draft *is* working, then it is time to share the draft with an editor.

The Initial Drafting Response Sheet

One instrument that guides both editor and writer is the Initial Drafting Response Sheet. This response sheet helps to guide the writer's efforts to expand and shape ideas and opinions so that they will be clearer and more complete for the reader or audience.*

*Much of the early work on response sheets for editors and writers was done by Roland K. Huff during many years of teaching writing and training teachers of writing.

Early versions of the response sheets included here were developed by Dana Elder, Paulette Scott, and Jean Hegland, who designed and field-tested these instruments at Eastern Washington University.

The term *nutshelling* as applied to writing was popularized by Linda Flower of Carnegie-Mellon University.

INITIAL DRAFTING RESPONSE SHEET

Author _____ Title _____

Date _____ Responder _____

NUTSHELLING: In 25 words or less, what is the focus of this piece of writing — what does the author want to communicate, and to whom is he or she writing?

FORMING:

1. What in this text doesn't belong in *this* piece of writing — extra points, inappropriate examples or quotations, extra talk? Circle these spots in the text; then write the page numbers of the marked places here and explain why they don't seem to belong.

2. Are there places where the writer should include more details, add examples, or address another major point? Put an asterisk (*) by these places in the text; then suggest here what additions might be appropriate.

3. Are there places in this piece of writing where what follows doesn't connect with what comes before — where the flow of the draft breaks? Identify these places with brackets in the text; then suggest here what the writer might do to mend these breaks.

Nutshelling: If the writer, or someone else, can't say what the initital draft is about in twenty-five words or less, then it's likely that the initial draft has no clear focus. The writer might be trying to do too much or might be confused about what he or she is attempting to communicate. When this happens, the writer should probably pick one part of the draft, or even one idea from the draft, and write a new initial draft. Experience suggests that it takes less work over the long run and the chances for success are greater if the writer writes another initial draft rather than tries to repair or salvage one that is not working.

1. Most initial drafts contain extra talk — words, sentences, or paragraphs that don't belong in *that* draft. These extras should be circled, and circled parts of the initial draft should be omitted in the next draft.
2. Very often a writer will present an opinion in a draft but will not support it with examples, details, or facts. Every opinion and every generalization needs to be supported. Look in the initial draft for those places where the writer needs to add support. Mark those places with an asterisk (*). The person completing the Initial Drafting Response Sheet should also suggest what kinds of support might be added.
3. The reader (audience) should always know how the paragraphs and larger sections of a draft are connected. Making the connections is part of the writer's job. The reader should mark with square brackets [ ] the places in the initial draft where he or she loses the writer's train of thought, the places where the reader "gets lost."

Two people should complete the Initial Drafting Response Sheet for each initial draft. One might be the writer, the other a friend of the writer or another student in the same class. When possible, a third reader is desirable. Then the writer should again set the draft aside and let it "incubate" or "cool off" for at least twenty-four hours.

Using the Initial Drafting Response Sheet

EXAMPLE 1:

Poverty

Poverty is growing as time progresses.* There are many reasons for poverty, and there are, also, different types of poverty. Therefore, people should be helping one another, but instead, it is every man for himself. People are getting so materialistic that it is sometimes hard for people to compete with one another.

I think it starts when people are young and playing with others. It starts out who has the latest toy. Or maybe who has the most clothes and in the fashion. Then it gets to who has the nicest car. The older one gets, the more it costs.*

What are people paying for? It is status, or how successful one is. It seems to be a game of money, also,

it's a way to get attention from
another one.

   Then there is the people who
gave up on the game. I recently
moved to down town Seattle. There is
a place where the dirty poor is.
People see you walk by, and they
asked you for some money because they
have to sleep out side in the cold.

   So people think they have it
ruff because they can't have a new
car. But if everyone could stop
wanting so many material things. I
think we wouldn't have such a big
problem in poverty.

                                   Jill B.

INITIAL DRAFTING RESPONSE SHEET

Author *Jill B.*   Title *Poverty*

Date *Spring 1988*   Responder *B. Williams*

NUTSHELLING: In 25 words or less, what is the focus of this piece of writing—what does the author want to communicate, and to whom is he or she writing?

People are too materialistic. Because they only think of themselves they can't see that other people are really in need. Written to people who only worry about themselves.

FORMING:

1. What in this text doesn't belong in *this* piece of writing—extra points, inappropriate examples or quotations, extra talk? Circle these spots in the text; then write the page numbers of the marked places here and explain why they don't seem to belong.

   1st paragraph, last sentence: Do you need this sentence?

2. Are there places where the writer should include more details, add examples, or address another major point? Put an asterisk (*) by these places in the text; then suggest here what additions might be appropriate.

   1st sentence: Can you add details to support this?
   2nd paragraph: I would add details and examples to each sentence here. This is an important part of your message.

3. Are there places in this piece of writing where what follows doesn't connect with what comes before—where the flow of the draft breaks? Identify these places with brackets in the text; then suggest here what the writer might do to mend these breaks.

(An editor could make many more comments at this stage of the process. For *this writer*, on *this draft*, the three suggestions made are enough to guide the writer toward a better draft.)

In response to the remarks on the preceding Initial Drafting Response Sheet, the author made the following changes.

Poverty

more people than ever are freezing to death because they have no homes. People who have always had jobs now dont have them, and the newspapers are full of articles about families trying to live on one person's job at a fast food restaurant.

Poverty is growing as time progresses.✱ There are many reasons for poverty, and there are, also, different types of poverty. Therefore, people should be helping one another, but instead, it is every man for himself. People are getting so materialistic that it is sometimes hard for people to compete with one another.

I think it starts when people are young and playing with others.

It starts out who has the latest toy. *like a "Rambo" doll or remote* Or maybe who has the ~~most~~ *control airplane* ~~clothes and in the fashion~~. Then it

best designer → *a BMW or Mercedes*
jeans or the gets to who has ~~the nicest car~~. The
most clothes, *to have better stuff than*
from nordstrom's older one gets, the more ~~it costs~~.
other people

It's like stuff is more important than what you do.

What are people paying for? It is status, or how successful one is. It seems to be a game of money, also,

i̱t's a way to get attention
from one another
~~from another one~~.

Then there is the people who
gave up on the game. I recently
moved to down town Seattle. There is
a place where the dirty poor is.
People see you walk by, and they
asked you for some money because they
have to sleep out side in the cold.

So people think they have it
ruff because they can't have a new
car. But if everyone could stop
wanting so many material things. I
think we wouldn't have such a big ⋏*poverty*
problem ~~in poverty~~.

                                     Jill B.

The following is the revision of the initial draft, with the
changes added by the writer. She decides, however, that the draft
can be even better. So she asks another person to act as editor and
complete an Initial Drafting Response Sheet for this revised
version.

                    Poverty

          Poverty is growing as time
progresses. More people than ever
are freezing to death because they
have no homes. People who have

always had jobs now don't have them,
and the newspapers are full of
articles about families trying to
live on one person's job at a
fastfood restaurant. There are many
reasons for poverty, and there are,
also, different types of poverty.
Therefore, people should be helping
one another, but instead, it is
every man for himself.

I think it starts when people
are young and playing with others.
It starts out who has the latest toy,
like a ''Rambo'' doll or a remote
control airplane. Or maybe who has
the best designer jeans or the most
clothes from Nordstroms. Then it
gets to who has a BMW or a Mercedes.
The older one gets, the more it costs
to have better stuff than other
people. It's like stuff is more
important than what you do.

What are people paying for? It
is status, or how successful one is.
It seems to be a game of money, also,
it's a way to get attention from one
another.

Then there is the people who
gave up on the game. I recently
moved to down town Seattle. There is
a place where the dirty poor is.
People see you walk by, and they
asked you for some money because they
have to sleep out side in the cold.

So people think they have it
ruff because they can't have a new
car. But if everyone could stop
wanting so many material things,* I
think we wouldn't have such a big
poverty problem.

                                    Jill B.

INITIAL DRAFTING RESPONSE SHEET

Author *Jill B.*   Title *Poverty*

Date *Spring 1988*   Responder *Teri F.*

NUTSHELLING: In 25 words or less, what is the focus of this piece of writing—what does the author want to communicate, and to whom is he or she writing?

A lrg reason for poverty is that people only think about things they want to have. Written to people who sometimes forget about others.

FORMING:

1. What in this text doesn't belong in *this* piece of writing—extra points, inappropriate examples or quotations, extra talk? Circle these spots in the text; then write the page numbers of the marked places here and explain why they don't seem to belong.

   3rd paragraph: Either develop this part or leave it out.

2. Are there places where the writer should include more details, add examples, or address another major point? Put an asterisk (*) by these places in the text; then suggest here what additions might be appropriate.

   Last paragraph: Develop this — how would not wanting so many things help with the poverty problem.

3. Are there places in this piece of writing where what follows doesn't connect with what comes before—where the flow of the draft breaks? Identify these places with brackets in the text; then suggest here what the writer might do to mend these breaks.

Using some of this second editor's advice, the writer did more revising.

Poverty

Poverty is growing as time progresses. More people than ever are freezing to death because they have no homes. People who have always had jobs now don't have them, and the newspapers are full of articles about families trying to live on one person's job at a fastfood restaurant. There are many reasons for poverty, and there are, also, different types of poverty. Therefore, people should be helping one another, but instead, it is every man for himself.

I think it starts when people are young and playing with others. It starts out who has the latest toy, like a "Rambo" doll or a remote control airplane. Or maybe who has the best designer jeans or the most clothes from Nordstroms. Then it gets to who has a BMW or a Mercedes.

The older one gets, the more it costs
to have better stuff than other
people. It's like stuff is more
important than what you do.

Then there is the people who
gave up on the game. I recently
moved to down town Seattle. There is
a place where the dirty poor is.
People see you walk by, and they
asked you for some money because they
have to sleep out side in the cold.

So people think they have it
ruff because they can't have a new
car. But if everyone could stop
wanting so many material things, I
think we wouldn't have such a big
poverty problem. People need to find
joy in doing things rather than
having things. Working with a child
in a big brother program might be
enjoyable. Instead of buying a
speed boat, a person could donate a
couple of hours one night a week to a
Boy Scout troop or a foodbank. It
might be that helping others feels

```
better than helping yourself to more

stuff.
```

```
Jill B.
```

This draft may not be perfect yet, but it is better than it was. By getting suggestions from others, the writer has made improvements on her essay and perhaps learned a little more about writing essays.

EXAMPLE #2:

```
Grandma's Driving

    It was a chilly fall morning, on

October 10, and I had a dentist

appointment that morning.  My

Grandma was to pick me up that

morning, and drive me to my dentist

appointment.  She finally pulled in

the driveway, almost taking out our

fence.  I always hated driving with

Grandma.  As I got in the car I

buckled my seat belt securely; she

took off, and this time she almost

took the mailbox off the post.  As we

were driving down the road she would

always drive almost on the curb, and

also when she would turn a corner she
```

would run over the curbs. We were
almost to the dentist; Grandma ran a
stop light,* but we finally got to the
dentist safely.

One reason elderly people
shouldn't drive is because their
eye-sight is not as good as it used
to be.* They do not drive the speed
limit and they usually go about 10
MPH under the speed limit. They also
always forget to turn on their turn
signals, and they just go right in
front of people thinking everyone
will stop for them. They also can't
hear that well.* Elderly people
always swerve when they drive. Then
they will finally realize what they
are doing and move back into their
lane slowly. When they pull into
parking places they never park
straight, and when they open their
doors they usually hit the other
cars, because they park so close to
them. They just don't pay attention
to what they are doing when they are
driving or parking.

There are alternatives that we can consider. Not all elderly people are like this, but all people 60 and over should take a driving, eye, and ear exam every 5 years to see if they still have the ability to drive, see, and hear. If they do not, then they can't have their licenses back, and the ones that pass the exams can drive for another 5 years, but they will need to take the exams again in 5 years, and every 5 years after that.

A lot of elderly people tend to lose their alertness after the age of 60. This causes their driving ability to leave them, and other people on the road to be nervous when they see elders driving. To cut down on accidents on the road caused by Senior Citizens, a mandatory exam should be given to them every 5 years. Although I love Grandma dearly, I love her better when she's baking cookies than when she's driving me around in her car.

Keri L.

INITIAL DRAFTING RESPONSE SHEET

Author _Keri L._ Title _Grandma's Driving_

Date _Spring 1988_ Responder _M. Casten's_

NUTSHELLING: In 25 words or less, what is the focus of this piece of writing — what does the author want to communicate, and to whom is he or she writing?

Senior citizens sometimes don't realize they don't drive well and something should be done about this. Written to people who have older drivers in their family.

FORMING:

1. What in this text doesn't belong in *this* piece of writing — extra points, inappropriate examples or quotations, extra talk? Circle these spots in the text; then write the page numbers of the marked places here and explain why they don't seem to belong.

   Last paragraph: You already said this.

2. Are there places where the writer should include more details, add examples, or address another major point? Put an asterisk (*) by these places in the text; then suggest here what additions might be appropriate.

   Last sentence; 1st paragraph: Add descriptive details. 1st sentence; 2nd paragraph: add descriptive details. Middle of 2nd paragraph: Add descriptive details.

3. Are there places in this piece of writing where what follows doesn't connect with what comes before — where the flow of the draft breaks? Identify these places with brackets in the text; then suggest here what the writer might do to mend these breaks.

Using the advice on the Initial Drafting Response Sheet, this writer produced the following revised draft.

```
Grandma's Driving

        It was a chilly fall morning, on
October 10, and I had a dentist
appointment that morning. My
Grandma was to pick me up that
morning, and drive me to my dentist
appointment. She finally pulled in
the driveway, almost taking out our
fence. I always hated driving with
Grandma. As I got in the car I
buckled my seat belt securely; she
took off, and this time she almost
took the mailbox off the post. As we
were driving down the road she would
always drive almost on the curb, and
also when she would turn a corner she
would run over the curbs. We were
almost to the dentist; Grandma ran a
stop light, cars started screeching
all around, and Grandma kept
driving, not even knowing what she
had done, but we finally got to the
dentist safely.
```

One reason elderly people
shouldn't drive is because their
eye-sight is not as good as it used
to be. They see things that are not
really there, or they don't see
things at all and run into things, or
people. They do not drive the speed
limit, and they usually go about 10
MPH under the speed limit. They also
always forget to turn on their turn
signals, and they just go right in
front of people thinking everyone
will stop for them. They also can't
hear that well, because when people
honk at them, they don't hear them
and they keep on doing what they're
doing. If they can hear, then they
just ignore people when they honk at
them, because they think they are
doing nothing wrong. Elderly people
always swerve when they drive
because their body shakes, and it
makes their steering wheel move all
over the place. They don't know that
they are shaking, and all of a sudden

they will be coming into the other lane. Then they will finally realize what they are doing and move back into their lane slowly. When they pull into parking places they never park straight, and when they open their doors they usually hit the other cars, because they park so close to them. They just don't pay attention to what they are doing when they are driving or parking.

A lot of elderly people tend to lose their alertness after the age of 60. This causes their driving ability to leave them, and other people on the road to be nervous when they see elders driving. To cut down on accidents on the road caused by Senior Citizens, a mandatory exam should be given to them every 5 years. Although I love Grandma dearly, I love her better when she's baking cookies than when she's driving me around in her car.

Keri L.

This essay could be revised at least one more time, but it is getting better. Note that the writer made some changes that the editor suggested *and* some of her own.

WRAPPING IT UP: Proofreading a Typed Draft of an Essay

After a draft is as good as the writer (with the help of several editors) can make it, the *writer* is responsible for "cleaning up" the grammar, spelling, typographical, and punctuation errors. Reading typed copy and identifying surface errors is called *proofreading*. In this book, responding to the content or form of a draft is called *editing*. Proofreading takes place after all the editing is completed. Once again, it is easier for writers to see someone else's errors than it is for them to see their own. For this reason, it is wise to trade typed drafts with someone else and share the task of finding errors. The actual repairs should be made by the writer once the errors are located. Ironically, most of the errors in a given draft are there not because the writer doesn't know the correct spelling or punctuation, but because he or she has not proofread carefully. Most instructors and professional editors prefer that writers correct, in pencil, the surface errors in their typed papers. Essays that have been drafted on a personal computer are even easier to proofread and repair. Some computer software will check spelling, but this software is not a substitute for careful proofreading. Writers should always proofread their essays whether they are typed on a typewriter or printed on a personal computer. Instructors should not be expected to "sweep up" after irresponsible writers.

What sometimes happens when students don't proofread carefully is that instructors try to teach students rules that the students already know. This can waste time. On the other hand, the responsible student who honestly doesn't know how to spell a word should consult a dictionary. The student who honestly does not understand a grammar or punctuation rule should consult the teacher or another student who seems to know the rules. As a general principle, a person who wants to learn can learn, and a person who does not care to learn will not.

This book, as mentioned in the introduction, is not about grammar. Many people believe that people have to write good essays before they worry about correct spelling, punctuation, and grammar. Still, it is very important for the *last draft* of an essay to be carefully checked for these things (proofread).

But there is good news here. Often when writers write essays that say what they really want to communicate, then they will want to make sure their essays are as close to perfect as they can make them. This includes fixing the spelling, grammar, and punctuation errors.

Most people need help with this. Writers who have been working with other writers can help each other make their essays as good as they can be. This is part, the last part, of the process of writing an essay.

There is more good news. People who write often and read regularly make fewer and fewer mistakes in grammar, punctuation, and spelling. Many individuals learn to spell by reading.

The point is that good writing is more important than good spelling. Learn to write first. Remember, too, that inaccurate spelling and grammar and typing errors interfere with communication and make the writer look irresponsible; so on that last typed version of your essay, get the help you need to find and correct such errors.

The following are some common strategies for proofreading a typed draft of an essay. Remember that most readers would rather see corrections in pencil on a typed or computer-printed draft than find those errors themselves.

1. Many individuals are better able to find surface errors in typed drafts if they can hear them. So read your draft aloud to someone or to a mirror and listen for errors.
2. It is helpful for the author to read his or her draft from right to

left across the page, looking at each word individually. This strategy is especially useful for finding spelling and typographical errors.

3. Many writers keep lists of words they have misspelled in the past. Then, when they are proofreading, they can check the words in their essays against their lists.

ACTIVITIES

A. *Working alone*

1. In ten minutes, write what you think the role of the ideal editor would be. What kinds of advice would be most useful to you? Where do you feel you need more help?

2. As honestly as possible, use the Initial Drafting Response Sheet on one of your essays. Focus your comments on how the essay can be improved.

3. On your draft, make some of the changes suggested in activity **A.2.**

B. *Working with others*

1. Discuss the concept of perfect writing. What would it include? What would it look like?

2. Read Student Draft #1 (pages 139–140). Then, with others, complete the Initial Drafting Response Sheet.

3. As a group, use the editorial advice you have just made on Student Draft #1 to guide you as you make improvements on the draft.

4. Repeat activities **B.2** and **B.3** on Student Draft #2 (pages 141–143).

5. Design your own response sheet; then apply it to either Student Draft #1, #2, or #3.

Each culture or community has
its own social problem. One of these
problems is the involvement of
people in illegal activities such as
smuggling, stealing and gambling.
In the community that I was raised,
the major social problem that affect
the people is smuggling.

My hometown, Kuala Perlis, is a
fisherman town. It is located at the
Northern part of Malaysia; almost at
the border of Thailand. Sixty-five
percent of people there are Malays,
30 percent are Chinese and the rest
are Indian and foreigner. The
smuggling activities usually
involve local people and the
foreigner who came from Thailand.
They smuggle drug, ciggarete and
goods from Thailand to Malaysia.
These smuggling activities are hard

to control because the smuggler
always disguise themselves as
fishermen.

These activities cause problem
in my hometown because it increases
the number of drug addicted among
young people. The smuggler bring a
lot of drugs especially cocaine and
heroine into my country because they
can gain a large profit. The people
who buy them then sell these drugs to
the local drug addicted. They will
try to influence young people who
have no job and uneducated to involve
in it. By doing these they can have a
lot of consumer.

There is not much can be done
with this problem in my community. A
lot of people realize that the
government should do something to
decrease this activity. The police
department at Kuala Perlis should
increase their work.

Salmi A.

STUDENT DRAFT #2:

I came from a small farming community in Southwestern Idaho. In the past few years there has been an increased number of farmers being arrested for growing marijuana. I feel these arrests are due to the instability of farming.

For the past several years farming has become a very difficult way of life. In the late 1970's and early 80's land value was at it's peak. Many farmers purchased land believing that the prices would only increase more. Still other farmers borrowed against their land, increasing their debt load tremendously. Then about 1982 we started into a recession. Banks began calling loans. Farmers tried to refinance, but found that land value had dropped so drastically that they owed more money against the land they owned than the land was worth.

Many farmers began to look for ways to save their farms. Many of theses farms had been in the family for many years. One such farm was homsteaded on in the late 1880's by Austrian immigrants.

In searching for new ways to raise the money needed to pay their ever increasing debt load a few farmers began to raise marijuana.

Marijuana if grown in the center of corn fields is a very noticeable crop to an aircraft flying overhead. These farmers began growing marijuana in the alkali weeds that grow beside the corn fields. Alkali is a weed that looks very similar to marijuana and can grow to heights of 10 to 12 feet.

Authorities became aware of the increased amount of marijuana and thus began a search. They increased the number of photographs being taken of fields. They also began giving large rewards for information leading to the arrest and conviction of anyone dealing with the raising or selling of marijuana.

Today I feel we must not condemn the farmers for what society or government has caused. We must find ways to help them meet their debts. Perhaps the government needs to place seals on the price of equipment they must purchase instead of the products they sale. If we do not help we may eventually find our country a very hungry country.

Barbara B.

STUDENT DRAFT #3:

Crime Pays in This Town

Crime pays in this area. To support yourself in crime is the average survival job of many citizens. In an area of extreme unemployment, large drop-out percentages, many teenage mothers, and not training for jobs available, the social problems here incite many citizens to have an underground market for ''goods'' in demand, whatever they may be.

Money is just part of the appeal for the poor or the white-collar crime. The bad funding and priorities of the city council have left the city practically defenseless with not enough police officers for investigation and too few prosecuting attorneys, once these ''citizens'' are caught. Rapists, burglars, and drug dealers know they will be released in a few hours, if they are ever caught by the

understaffed police department.
There are files and files of cases
waiting to be tried, some several
years old, due to the lack of lawyers
and judges. In the meantime, the
dealers, fencers, burglars are
"working" full time. What is the
incentive to stop when the mayor
chooses to spend city money to fly to
China and Russia instead of funding
for the prosecution and police
departments.

The amount of money to be made is
quite a lot in stealing and growing
pot, a main occupation in this area.
Instead of choosing jobs for $3.25
per hour if you're lucky enough to
have the clothing, training, and bus
fare, these citizens use their
survival skills which is not an
hourly rate. Many dealers make
thousands of dollars selling,
growing, distributing drugs either
grown themselves or by other
citizens. Burglary is big business
in the area to where whole families

generation to generation have a
hierarchy on that crime, stealing,
fencing, trading of drugs. It's a
whole economy of goods and drugs.
They have the vocational training
for their jobs and they are proud of
making money, instead of starving.
This is usually the only training
available to the forgotten citizens.

Most citizens in crime develop a
sense of proudness about their
jobs. A man is proud to provide for
his family, a typical feeling no
matter how he does this. In this
town, this applies to women as well.
The self esteem is usually very low,
due to lack of education, training,
and a family started very early in
life. To know you can't support
yourself or your family can start
many social and family problems. To
be able to have money in your pocket,
to have the macho or female egotism,
and a sense of self esteem for once
in your life feels great. Crime pays
psychologically too for most

citizens. This is important for everyone and in the area the cycle of this kind of confusion or perspective on life continues generation to generation. This is a great place but caters to the criminal citizens instead of the citizen victims. Crime pays here and the word is spreading.

Kitty H.

Chapter

8 MAKING IT EVEN BETTER
Rewriting Revisited

5-15 *Larson* Chronicle Features, 1981

"Okay, okay, okay . . . . Everyone
just calm down and we'll try this
thing one more time."

Here comes some tough talk. Many people are so sure that the
only good essay is a finished essay that they like anything they
write. I have heard people say things like, "If you don't understand what I'm writing, that's your problem." The truth is that
making sure the reader understands is *the writer's* responsibility;
it is the writer's job.

So this is what happens. A writer produces an initial draft. The writer or somebody else reads the initial draft and believes that it is difficult or even impossible to understand. When this happens, the writer sometimes needs to start again. This isn't always easy, but it is often wise.

This also happens. A writer writes a good initial draft, gets some advice from a reader, and then uses some of this input to make a revised draft that is better than the initial draft. Good. But this second draft still has some problems. It needs more examples. It may need another whole part. This happens all the time. Most essays should be revised at least twice. The good news is that generally the more times you rewrite an essay, the better the essay. Many people believe that the more times you write about a particular subject, even if each time you write a completely different essay, the better the writing will be.

There is more good news. The more you rewrite, the better you get at rewriting. Doing *is* learning. You learn to rewrite only by rewriting. Plan on it. Give yourself time to do it.

AUDIENCE DRAFTING

What follows are some strategies to help make a good essay even better. These next steps are not always necessary. If the revising has been honest and thorough, then the writer may not need to do any audience drafting. However, if what a person is writing is *very* important, that person might consider doing the additional steps. For most purposes, a good initial draft that has been revised twice will be good enough. On the other hand, if a person wants a challenge and wants to make the essay the very best it can be, he or she should try audience drafting. From one perspective, audience drafting is double-checking your rhetoric. What follows is one way to do this additional rewriting. The Audience Drafting Response Sheet (pages 152–153) is complicated. Writers who only have time to complete parts of it should do as much as possible. It is not necessary to do it all. As a general rule, the more of it the writer completes, the better.

The writer, having completed an initial draft (or two or three), should again lay the manuscript aside for at least a day. Most people cannot see problems in a draft they have just written. Initial drafts vary in their levels of completeness. Some are ninety-nine percent finished; others need more work. Most can benefit from one more step—audience drafting.

The reader will remember that Chapter 3 of this text emphasizes the role of thinking about the intended audience from the very start of the writing process. Good writers keep their thoughts about their proposed audience in mind while writing. Communication is always communication *with someone.* Audience drafting is the process of drafting an essay to better meet the needs of the reader or audience. The Audience Drafting Response Sheet is one possible list of considerations for audience drafting.

AUDIENCE DRAFTING RESPONSE SHEET

Author _____ Title _____

Responder _____ Date _____

NUTSHELLING: In 25 words or less, identify and describe as specifically as possible the intended audience for this paper.

AUDIENCE/TEXT RELATIONSHIP:

1. *Introduction:* What information, examples, or statements does the present introduction include that will attract the attention of the audience? What might be added or deleted?

2. *Middle of the Essay:* Given that all of the ideas in the initial draft are supported by specific facts and examples, what other facts or examples would be more appropriate or more interesting to this particular audience? Are there other parts that this audience might expect to see in this essay?

3. *Conclusion:* Does the present conclusion address the concerns of the intended audience and leave that audience feeling like the essay is complete? What might be added, deleted, or rewritten to better meet the needs of the audience?

AUDIENCE/LANGUAGE RELATIONSHIP (optional):

1. Circle three words in the text that seem inappropriate for this audience, and suggest here two or more alternative choices.

2. Bracket two places in the text where the sentences could be longer, shorter, or combined with other sentences to make the meaning clearer and the style more graceful. Then suggest here some alternative sentences.

Using the Audience Drafting Response Sheet

Nutshelling: As mentioned previously, some people will say the audience for a draft is the general public or all college students. The general public is another way of saying everybody is the audience. The audience should *always* be more specific. All college students is also too general an audience to guide the writer in his or her thinking and writing. Usually the more specific the audience, the better. Many people will write to a particular person — a state senator, a high-school teacher, a brother, or a close friend. A reader (other than the writer) should be able to read an initial draft and imagine who the intended audience for the draft is. A word of caution. Quite often the audience that the writer envisions when starting an initial draft is not the audience to whom that person ends up writing. This is normal. The important thing is knowing who the intended audience is for the draft that the writer has actually written.

Audience/Text Relationship:

Introductions: Every essay needs some sort of introduction that (1) lets the reader know what the essay will be about (issue), (2) includes the writer's opinion(s) on that issue, and (3) catches the reader's attention by alerting him or her to why the writer is writing about the issue. The introduction should therefore be reviewed late in the process to see if these three things have been accomplished.

One way to check this is to look back at the communication situation triangle you made while preparing to write. Look particularly at your notes about the relationship between the issue and the audience. If the audience has changed during the writing process, you should consider making another triangle.

How can you be sure of how to introduce your essay before you know what your essay will say and look like? The answer is that you can't. Sometimes the process of writing what you really mean changes what you think you think, and your original introduction may no longer fit the essay you have written. Sometimes writers know so well what they will write that the first version of an introduction is adequate; usually it is not.

So let us say that you have written an essay and then rewritten it twice. It says what *you* want to say. You then go back and read your whole essay out loud, either to someone else or to a mirror, and then you ask yourself the following questions:

1. What is this essay really about?

You might discover at this point that you thought the essay was about how much trouble it is to have a teenager in the house, but it is actually about what it takes to be a good parent of a teenager. Maybe the essay that started out to be about that low-paying, highly stressful job you had last summer has turned into an essay about how fulltime employees discriminate against part-time employees. The point is that you often will not know the direction of the essay until it is written.

The key is being honest. Try to read your essay as though someone else had written it; what is this other person's essay about?

2. What is the writer's opinion toward this issue?

Here again, try to imagine that you are not the author. If you had seen this essay in a newspaper or magazine and just read it for the first time, what would your impression be of the writer's opinion? Remember that an essay *is* a writer's ideas and opinions and some of the reasons behind them.

3. Why is this writer writing about this?

Or, in other words, what got this author started on this topic? Different stimuli get people started on writing projects. A quotation from a politician's speech could be part of the introduction to an essay about state support of education. A sentence from an article in a news magazine or some frightening statistics about the nutritional value of fast foods might be included in the first paragraph of an essay about fast foods.

Life experiences are excellent starting points. Everyone sees squat, brown, beer bottles and aluminum cans by the sides of public highways. A writer could certainly describe these in the introduction to an essay about drinking beer and driving.

Some people call this part of an introduction *the hook*. This is a fishing metaphor; once the writer has hooked the reader, he or she can reel that reader in. Others think of it as a *bridge*. The writer can include a bridge that will help a reader to understand quickly and easily why that writer is writing that particular essay. When writers include a shocking statistic, they hope readers will find it as shocking as they do. When they mention empty beer bottles by the side of the road, they hope readers will think, "Yeah, I've seen those, and they're ugly."

A word of caution. Your bridge doesn't have to be what really got you started on the essay project. Realistically speaking, you may be writing about an issue found within an assigned subject. But, even then, why not include some likely reason for writing the essay you have written?

If your introduction already answers the three key questions, leave the introduction alone. If any question remains unanswered, rewrite the introduction.

Middle of the Essay: A reader (audience) will find examples that he or she can identify with very powerful. In an essay about health and fitness written to a retired construction contractor, a writer might draw examples from or comparisons to the construction industry. In this case, having a complete physical examination by the family doctor might be compared to getting a building permit to remodel a suite of offices in an existing building.

Another concern here is the units of the essay. It is useful to outline the body of a draft at this time. What are its units? What does each cluster of related paragraphs contribute to the essay? Is there another unit that your intended audience would want or expect to see? If so, write it and include it in your essay.

Conclusions: Good conclusions are fairly easy to write. A common pitfall, however, is not doing enough with the conclusion. It happens all the time. A writer has worked hard on an essay, has struggled to make the essay as good as he or she can make it, but ends the essay with a single sentence, such as "Poverty would end if everybody cared more." This statement may or may not be true, but it is not much of a conclusion. The conclusion of an essay is the writer's last chance to communicate with his or her audience. It needs to be more than the last gasp of a tired writer.

So what kinds of things can go into a conclusion? Fortunately, the writer has many options. The section on pages 158–160 covers some of them.

Audience/Language Relationship: Late in the process of writing an essay, it is advisable to look at word choice (diction). Is the vocabulary used in the draft too simple or too complex for the intended audience? A good rule of thumb when choosing between a simple term and a more sophisticated one is to use the simple one. Of course, a person presenting himself or herself as an expert biologist to an audience of biologists should use the terminology, or jargon, shared by people in that profession.

As a general rule, sentence length in a draft should vary. The writer should employ a mixture of short, medium, and long sentences. Such a mixture is easier to read.

As with the Initial Drafting Response Sheet, at least two people should complete the Audience Drafting Response Sheet on a given draft. Here again, allowing time to pass between the completion of the Audience Drafting Response Sheets and the rewriting of the draft is important. The writer should then review the Response Sheets and make changes in the draft. The newly revised draft should be typed and proofread. Once again, proofreading is the writer's job and not the teacher's.

RESOURCES FOR ESSAY CONCLUSIONS

The following resources for essay conclusions are divided into four categories. The items discussed are resources that a writer *might include*; nobody would put all of them into one conclusion, but a writer could use at least three in any conclusion to an essay. The writer can include sentences that make the writer look like a reasonable person, sentences that reinforce the ideas and opinions included in the essay, sentences that appeal to the emotions of the reader, and recommendations to the reader for further thought or action.

Making the Writer Look Reasonable

Two ways for the writer to make him- or herself look like a reasonable person are admitting that the writer doesn't know everything about the issue discussed and pointing out places where people who don't agree with that writer's opinion are thinking clearly and accurately. A third way is to mention values shared by the writer and the reader.

1. For example, a writer who has written an essay about traffic safety might write, "Of course I don't know everything there is to know about how the Highway Commission determines a "safe" speed limit for a particular stretch of highway, but. . . ." By admitting that his or her knowledge is limited, the writer looks more reasonable.
2. The writer who argues in an essay that alcohol is the biggest health threat faced by young people today might write, "Those who think drinking helps people deal with stress are probably right part of the time." By admitting that opinions other than the writer's might have some validity, the writer sounds more mature.
3. Another resource for writers of conclusions is shared values or goals. For example, almost everybody in this country thinks saving money is important. In an essay, once again about

traffic safety, the writer might mention in the essay's conclusion that good driving habits save everybody money by keeping insurance rates down.

Reinforcing Opinions Included in the Essay

There are several ways to reinforce your opinions. The easiest is reading back through the essay, picking out the two or three most important ideas, then simply mentioning them again in the conclusion. For shorter essays, this kind of repetition is usually not necessary.

Another way to reinforce opinions presented in an essay is to quote a recognized authority. In an essay on traffic safety, the writer could quote a state patrol officer. In an essay about education, the writer could quote a state senator or the Secretary of Education for the United States of America. The quotation has to fit the essay, of course; the writer has to find and choose an appropriate quotation.

A third way to strengthen or reinforce an essay's conclusion is to mention and then refute an argument made by someone who disagrees with the writer. It is more effective to suggest that those who disagree with the writer are shortsighted or misinformed rather than stupid or inferior. To disagree effectively, the writer both acknowledges other people's opinions and makes himself or herself look reasonable.

Appealing to the Emotions of the Reader

Everyone has read and heard these kinds of appeals. Candidates for offices in government talk about what is "good for America." They are appealing to the emotions clustered around the term "patriotism." When advertisers say that "Good mothers choose" this or that product, they are aware that every parent wants to be a good parent.

In an essay conclusion, the writer *might* include an appeal to emotions. He or she might write something about how this essay supports an important tradition or about how applying the thinking presented in the essay will make life better in the future for all of us.

Recommendations for Further Thought or Action

This is an excellent resource for an essay conclusion. When someone really communicates in an essay, that person will want readers to *do* something after having read it.

Such recommendations, however, should be both specific and realistic. A writer should not, for example, end an essay about child abuse with the statement, "Child abuse would end if everybody cared more." This is too general. The writer might, on the other hand, direct readers toward a good book or article on the subject and provide enough specific information so that readers could find these additional readings. The writer might also recommend some volunteer work, once again including specific information; the names and addresses of local organizations that help children would be appropriate.

Many times essay writers will advise readers to write to government officials. Here again, names, titles, and addresses of these officials make the advice stronger and easier to act on. Remember to ask of your intended audience only those things that they will be able to do.

There are other resources for essay conclusions, but these are some of the best. Once again, the writer should use two or three of these resources in any given conclusion. Remember to choose the resources that fit *your essay* and *your audience*. Conclusions are usually not places to start whole new arguments that support the writer's opinions. If while writing your conclusion you come up with another major point, put it in the body of your essay. Writing *is* rewriting, and it is always wise to take some extra time to make an essay better.

NOTE TO THE READER ON
MULTIPLE-STEP DRAFTING

All of this rewriting may seem like too much work the first time you think about it. Nobody said writing essays was easy. The good news is that once you try these strategies, you may find that you like them. Better still, some of them will help you to write better essays. Don't expect to do these steps well the first time you try them. It doesn't work that way. It is advisable to do all these steps on at least three different essay projects before you decide whether they work for you. After you have tried them three times, you might find you don't need them all. It is likely that some will work for you and some won't. Use the ones that work for you.

ACTIVITIES

A. *Working with others*

1. Make enough copies of an article from a newspaper or news magazine so that each member of your writing group has one. As a group, look at the article's introduction. Does it (1) identify the essay's issue, (2) suggest the writer's opinion, and (3) give an idea why the writer is writing this essay? Can you, as a group, make improvements on the introduction?

2. Look at the conclusion to the same article. What resources has the writer used? Are there others that the writer could have used? Rewrite the conclusion to this essay.

3. Discuss other kinds of resources that a writer might consider when writing a conclusion to an essay. Make a list of these resources.

4. Exchange initial drafts of essays with another person in your writing group. Complete all or parts of the Audience Drafting Response Sheet on one another's essays.

5. Find an article or an editorial in a newspaper, and complete the Audience Drafting Response Sheet on it.

B. *Working alone*

1. Rewrite the introduction of an essay you have written.

2. Rewrite the introduction to someone else's essay.

3. Rewrite some of the examples and details in one of your essays to match better the needs and interests of your intended audience.

4. Choose one of the essay drafts included in this book, and revise the introduction and conclusion of that essay using some of the suggestions in this chapter.

5. Take an essay you have written and revise the introduction and the conclusion using some of the suggestions in this chapter.

6. Complete the Audience Drafting Response Sheet on the best essay you have written while using this book; then rewrite the essay one more time.

LETTER TO THE STUDENT

Learning to Speak and Write
Standard American English

© 1985 Universal Press Syndicate

*"Look out, Thak! It's
a . . . a . . . Dang! Never can
pronounce those things!"*

Dear Student:

There is a larger issue here. One part of being educated is speaking and writing Standard American English. Whether it is fair or unfair, people tend to judge one another on how they speak, and they certainly judge one another on how they write.

Yes, in different regions and communities, people speak the English language differently. In many places Standard American

English is not spoken. In a certain town in Washington State a native might ask another person why he or she holds a particular opinion by asking "How come?" People know what "How come?" means, but it sounds uneducated to an educated listener. In this same town people say "hunnerd" when they mean "hundred." A person might say "I gotta hunnerd dollars." In Standard American English, the same meaning would be communicated by the sentence "I have a hundred dollars." A person in this town might say, "Ya gotta wanna work good." That same sentence in Standard American English would be, "You have to want to work well." The point is that *how* you say it is nearly as important as *what* you say.

Expressions that are not Standard American English are, in some communication situations, perceived as verbal clues that indicate fewer years of formal education and a lower socioeconomic status. Standard American English is the language of published writing in the United States. It is often called the *prestige dialect* of English because it is shared by those who have social and economic power.

People who want to gain social and economic power, those who want that kind of prestige, have to learn to speak and write Standard American English. The following are four notions for the interested learner to keep in mind while accomplishing this goal:

1. An individual has to choose to learn the prestige dialect. This learning can only be accomplished through sustained attention and effort. In many ways it is like learning a foreign language. When learning Spanish, for example, one learns not only the vocabulary but the accepted forms of expression. To speak Spanish well, one must gain an understanding of the culture that uses Spanish. Standard American English is the language spoken and written in colleges, the professions, business, and the media; people in these fields speak it and expect to hear it spoken and see it written by their peers. People who choose to pursue college educations or to educate themselves choose to master Standard American English. They cannot choose otherwise.

Extensive reading is essential to this learning process. So is learning and applying the rules of grammar to one's own spoken and written English. Like any language, Standard American English takes most people several years to master.

2. On the positive side, people who master Standard American English do not forget the other dialects of English they know. Many people, some of them students, are concerned that by learning to speak and write Standard American English they will lose access to comfortable communication with family members and friends who have not mastered those standards. This is not a real danger. A person who learns a foreign language does not forget how to speak English in the process.

There are times when it is better to use your native dialect. The primary purpose of language is communication. Communication is accomplished more easily when those communicating are speaking the same language, so speaking Standard American English in a cowboy bar might not be appropriate. In some situations, expressions like "Howdy" and "Gonna go fishin'" fit right in. In a bank, however, or on a college campus, Standard American English is the rule. Educated Americans often speak two or more kinds of English.

3. One characteristic of people who are in the process of mastering Standard American English is a tendency to correct other people's spoken English. It is very tempting to do so, but the language learner should keep two important principles in mind: (a) there is no necessary correlation between Standard American English and intelligence; and (b) as a general rule, correcting other people's spoken language is considered impolite.

In an educational environment — a high school or community college or university — correcting another person's grammar or pronunciation is sometimes appropriate. Teachers, for example, often feel free to make such corrections; they perceive these corrections as important parts of their jobs. Students, too, in educational settings, should help one another in the process of learning to speak Standard American English correctly.

When possible, it is always better to make such corrections *privately.* Embarrassing people is not the same as teaching them. Therefore, outside of educational environments, one should not correct other people's grammar. One should not, for example, correct Uncle Joe when he says his car "runs good." He knows what he means, and he has the right to say what he means any way he likes.

4. Parents and people who will become parents have a special obligation to learn to speak and write Standard American English. Children who grow up in households where Standard American English is spoken often do better in school and, many people believe, in their careers. Parents who read more speak better. Studies suggest a very high correlation between a parent's or two parents' reading habits and their children's performance in school. The more a child sees mom and dad read, the more important reading becomes for that child.

Children, as every parent knows, learn more from what they see their parent or parents *do* than from what their parents tell them. I see evidence for this often. A friend told me recently that she has four children. She is now halfway through a degree program at a university. Her two oldest children, who did not see her reading, writing, and studying, did not do well in school. They did not value education. The two children who are still at home, the two who have seen her working on school assignments these last two years, are already doing better in school than ever before — much better than their older siblings ever did.

There is a lesson here, and an opportunity. *Telling* one's children that education is important is not enough. A parent has to *show* them. People's lives are like essays. Their children see the details of their lives — sometimes better than the parents themselves do. Parents are the examples from which their children learn. Parents should not tell children to respect teachers if those parents don't respect teachers; they should not tell their children to read and write if they themselves don't read and write. It is as simple *and* as complex as that. Just as parents can't help but love their children, they cannot avoid teaching them.

So what does all this have to do with good grammar and good writing? The two are certainly related. Good grammar does not simply come to a person as a gift. Nor can people read a grammar handbook once and learn all they need to know. People learn grammar like they learn to write or to play a violin. People learn by reading. They learn by listening, and they learn by studying. Most of all they learn by doing, by practicing. The best way to learn anything is to use all of these learning aids. By reading, listening, studying, and practicing, even the most difficult subject or skill can be mastered.

ACTIVITIES

A. *Working with others*

1. Discuss how you feel when somebody corrects your grammar. When are such corrections helpful? In what circumstances do you feel such corrections are inappropriate?
2. With your fellow writers, discuss the following: (a) Are there good reasons for learning to speak and write Standard American English? What are they? (b) Is Standard American English the prestige dialect of the United States? Can you think of examples to support your answer? (c) When, for instance, do grammar errors get in the way of communication?

B. *Working alone*

1. Are there words or expressions you use that are not Standard American English? If so, make a brief list of them. Then write down the same ideas in Standard American English.
2. Look over the writing you have done in this course. Do you often make the same kinds of grammar errors? Decide what you need to do to get help with these problems; then get that help.

AFTERWORD

After years of writing and teaching writing, I find I cannot just end this book; I have to write a brief conclusion. Thinking about my intended audience, there is one final point I feel a need to reinforce. I will end as I began, with an anecdote.

Last spring, in a grocery store, I ran into a man who had completed a freshman composition course I had taught seven years before. He smiled with his whole face when he saw me. We stood together in the checkout line.

After some chat about the weather and how life was treating each of us, I asked him, "Jim, do you ever use any of those prewriting strategies and response sheets we worked with in that course we did together?"

"No, Dana," he said. "But I've used yours as models and made my own. Now when I write I use the ones *I have made.*"

In all the years I have taught, I have not received a better compliment.

INDEX

INITIAL DRAFTING RESPONSE SHEET

Author _____ Title _____

Date _____ Responder _____

NUTSHELLING: In 25 words or less, what is the focus of this piece of writing — what does the author want to communicate, and to whom is he or she writing?

FORMING:

1. What in this text doesn't belong in *this* piece of writing — extra points, inappropriate examples or quotations, extra talk? Circle these spots in the text; then write the page numbers of the marked places here and explain why they don't seem to belong.

2. Are there places where the writer should include more details, add examples, or address another major point? Put an asterisk (*) by these places in the text; then suggest here what additions might be appropriate.

3. Are there places in this piece of writing where what follows doesn't connect with what comes before — where the flow of the draft breaks? Identify these places with brackets in the text; then suggest here what the writer might do to mend these breaks.

INITIAL DRAFTING RESPONSE SHEET

Author _____ Title _____

Date _____ Responder _____

NUTSHELLING: In 25 words or less, what is the focus of this piece of writing—what does the author want to communicate, and to whom is he or she writing?

FORMING:

1. What in this text doesn't belong in *this* piece of writing—extra points, inappropriate examples or quotations, extra talk? Circle these spots in the text; then write the page numbers of the marked places here and explain why they don't seem to belong.

2. Are there places where the writer should include more details, add examples, or address another major point? Put an asterisk (*) by these places in the text; then suggest here what additions might be appropriate.

3. Are there places in this piece of writing where what follows doesn't connect with what comes before—where the flow of the draft breaks? Identify these places with brackets in the text; then suggest here what the writer might do to mend these breaks.

INITIAL DRAFTING RESPONSE SHEET

Author _____ Title _____

Date _____ Responder _____

NUTSHELLING: In 25 words or less, what is the focus of this piece of writing — what does the author want to communicate, and to whom is he or she writing?

FORMING:

1. What in this text doesn't belong in *this* piece of writing — extra points, inappropriate examples or quotations, extra talk? Circle these spots in the text; then write the page numbers of the marked places here and explain why they don't seem to belong.

2. Are there places where the writer should include more details, add examples, or address another major point? Put an asterisk (*) by these places in the text; then suggest here what additions might be appropriate.

3. Are there places in this piece of writing where what follows doesn't connect with what comes before — where the flow of the draft breaks? Identify these places with brackets in the text; then suggest here what the writer might do to mend these breaks.

INITIAL DRAFTING RESPONSE SHEET

Author _____ Title _____

Date _____ Responder _____

NUTSHELLING: In 25 words or less, what is the focus of this piece of writing—what does the author want to communicate, and to whom is he or she writing?

FORMING:

1. What in this text doesn't belong in *this* piece of writing—extra points, inappropriate examples or quotations, extra talk? Circle these spots in the text; then write the page numbers of the marked places here and explain why they don't seem to belong.

2. Are there places where the writer should include more details, add examples, or address another major point? Put an asterisk (*) by these places in the text; then suggest here what additions might be appropriate.

3. Are there places in this piece of writing where what follows doesn't connect with what comes before—where the flow of the draft breaks? Identify these places with brackets in the text; then suggest here what the writer might do to mend these breaks.

AUDIENCE DRAFTING RESPONSE SHEET

Author _____ Title _____

Responder _____ Date _____

NUTSHELLING: In 25 words or less, identify and describe as specifically as possible the intended audience for this paper.

AUDIENCE/TEXT RELATIONSHIP:

1. *Introduction:* What information, examples, or statements does the present introduction include that will attract the attention of the audience? What might be added or deleted?

2. *Middle of the Essay:* Given that all of the ideas in the initial draft are supported by specific facts and examples, what other facts or examples would be more appropriate or more interesting to this particular audience? Are there other parts that this audience might expect to see in this essay?

3. *Conclusion:* Does the present conclusion address the concerns of the intended audience and leave that audience feeling like the essay is complete? What might be added, deleted, or rewritten to better meet the needs of the audience?

AUDIENCE/LANGUAGE RELATIONSHIP (optional):

1. Circle three words in the text that seem inappropriate for this audience, and suggest here two or more alternative choices.

2. Bracket two places in the text where the sentences could be longer, shorter, or combined with other sentences to make the meaning clearer and the style more graceful. Then suggest here some alternative sentences.

AUDIENCE DRAFTING RESPONSE SHEET

Author _____ Title _____

Responder _____ Date _____

NUTSHELLING: In 25 words or less, identify and describe as specifically as possible the intended audience for this paper.

AUDIENCE/TEXT RELATIONSHIP:

1. *Introduction:* What information, examples, or statements does the present introduction include that will attract the attention of the audience? What might be added or deleted?

2. *Middle of the Essay:* Given that all of the ideas in the initial draft are supported by specific facts and examples, what other facts or examples would be more appropriate or more interesting to this particular audience? Are there other parts that this audience might expect to see in this essay?

3. *Conclusion:* Does the present conclusion address the concerns of the intended audience and leave that audience feeling like the essay is complete? What might be added, deleted, or rewritten to better meet the needs of the audience?

AUDIENCE/LANGUAGE RELATIONSHIP (optional):

1. Circle three words in the text that seem inappropriate for this audience, and suggest here two or more alternative choices.

2. Bracket two places in the text where the sentences could be longer, shorter, or combined with other sentences to make the meaning clearer and the style more graceful. Then suggest here some alternative sentences.

AUDIENCE DRAFTING RESPONSE SHEET

Author _____ Title _____

Responder _____ Date _____

NUTSHELLING: In 25 words or less, identify and describe as specifically as possible the intended audience for this paper.

AUDIENCE/TEXT RELATIONSHIP:

1. *Introduction:* What information, examples, or statements does the present introduction include that will attract the attention of the audience? What might be added or deleted?

2. *Middle of the Essay:* Given that all of the ideas in the initial draft are supported by specific facts and examples, what other facts or examples would be more appropriate or more interesting to this particular audience? Are there other parts that this audience might expect to see in this essay?

3. *Conclusion:* Does the present conclusion address the concerns of the intended audience and leave that audience feeling like the essay is complete? What might be added, deleted, or rewritten to better meet the needs of the audience?

AUDIENCE/LANGUAGE RELATIONSHIP (optional):

1. Circle three words in the text that seem inappropriate for this audience, and suggest here two or more alternative choices.

2. Bracket two places in the text where the sentences could be longer, shorter, or combined with other sentences to make the meaning clearer and the style more graceful. Then suggest here some alternative sentences.

AUDIENCE DRAFTING RESPONSE SHEET

Author _____ Title _____

Responder _____ Date _____

NUTSHELLING: In 25 words or less, identify and describe as specifically as possible the intended audience for this paper.

AUDIENCE/TEXT RELATIONSHIP:
1. *Introduction:* What information, examples, or statements does the present introduction include that will attract the attention of the audience? What might be added or deleted?

2. *Middle of the Essay:* Given that all of the ideas in the initial draft are supported by specific facts and examples, what other facts or examples would be more appropriate or more interesting to this particular audience? Are there other parts that this audience might expect to see in this essay?

3. *Conclusion:* Does the present conclusion address the concerns of the intended audience and leave that audience feeling like the essay is complete? What might be added, deleted, or rewritten to better meet the needs of the audience?

AUDIENCE/LANGUAGE RELATIONSHIP (optional):

1. Circle three words in the text that seem inappropriate for this audience, and suggest here two or more alternative choices.

2. Bracket two places in the text where the sentences could be longer, shorter, or combined with other sentences to make the meaning clearer and the style more graceful. Then suggest here some alternative sentences.